Your Best Speech Ever
Delivery Workbook

by J.R. Steele

Published by, The International Public Speaking Institute
Fort Lauderdale, FL 2018

For more information contact: www.ipublicspeakingi.com

Cover and graphic design by Amy Parker
www.apdesignworks.com

ISBN: 978-1-947450-02-8

First Edition: January 2018

"Feel free to share this – just don't try to pass it off as your own!
If you enjoy this book, I really hope you'll do me the favor of leaving a review.
You can connect with me jr@yourbestspeechever.com

10 9 8 7 6 5 4 3 2 1

Delivery Workbook

Table of Contents

How to Use This Workbook

This workbook is designed to correspond directly to the book, *Your Best Speech Ever*. All of the interactions including the sample speeches at the end are here in the exact order as the text. At the end of this workbook there is an Appendix which provided feedback sheets and forms to support your improvement cycle, so you can continue to deliver your best speech ever.

> There are two types of speakers: those that are nervous and those that are liars.
>
> *– Mark Twain*

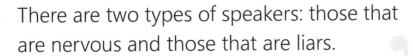

Chapter 1:
Forget Spiders, Snakes and Claustrophobia, Public Speaking Freaks Us Out

Objectives

By the end of this chapter you should be able to:

1. Describe how Dorothy and her friends facing the Great Oz can help us face an audience with control.

2. Identify your physical response to speaking in public.

3. Explain how what we feel differs from how we react and respond.

4. Identify methods to reduce the use of filler words when speaking in public.

5. Describe a communication theory that helps explain why the fear/anxiety exists.

1.1 A Lesson From Oz

Question: What is the lesson we can learn from Dorothy and her friends about what to do when you experience anxiety in the face of the unknown?

   a. Trust the unknown, embrace the experience.

   b. Feed the fear of the unknown by incorrectly perceiving they have special powers, thus giving them control.

   c. Remember that both parties are the same and are equally anxious.

   d. Don't ever trust anyone except yourself.

1.2 How Much Public Speaking Anxiety Do You Experience?

Instructions: Personal Report of Public Speaking Anxiety

This instrument is composed of thirty-four statements concerning feelings about communicating with other people. Indicate the degree to which the statements apply to you by marking whether you (1) strongly agree, (2) agree, (3) are undecided, (4) disagree, or (5) strongly disagree with each statement. Work quickly; record your first impression.

Note: You can take this test online at www.speechformula.com. Create a profile and measure your anxiety.

1.   While preparing to give a speech, I feel tense and nervous.

2.   I feel tense when I see the words "speech" and "public speech" on a course outline when studying.

3.   My thoughts become confused and jumbled when I am giving a speech.

4.   Right after giving a speech I feel that I have had a pleasant experience.

5.   I get anxious when I think about a speech coming up.

6.   I have no fear of giving a speech.

7.   Although I am nervous just before starting a speech, I soon settle down after starting and feel calm and comfortable.

8.   I look forward to giving a speech.

9.   When the instructor announces a speaking assignment in class, I can feel myself getting tense.

10.   My hands tremble when I am giving a speech.

11.   I feel relaxed when I am giving a speech.

12.   I enjoy preparing for a speech.

13.   I am in constant fear of forgetting what I prepared to say.

14.   I get anxious if someone asks me something about my topic that I do not know.

15.   I face the prospect of giving a speech with confidence.

16.   I feel that I am in complete possession of myself while giving a speech.

17.   My mind is clear when giving a speech.

18.   I do not dread giving a speech.

19.   I perspire just before starting a speech.

20.   My heart beats very fast just as I start a speech.

21.   I experience considerable anxiety while sitting in the room just before my speech starts.

22.   Certain parts of my body feel very tense and rigid while giving a speech.

23.   Realizing that only a little time remains in a speech makes me very tense and anxious.

24.   While giving a speech, I know I can control my feelings of tension and stress.

25.   I breathe faster just before starting a speech.

26. I feel comfortable and relaxed in the hour or so just before giving a speech.

27. I do poorer on speeches because I am anxious.

28. I feel anxious when the teacher announces the date of a speaking assignment.

29. When I make a mistake while giving a speech, I find it hard to concentrate on the parts that follow.

30. During an important speech I experience a feeling of helplessness building up inside me.

31. I have trouble falling asleep the night before a speech.

32. My heart beats very fast while I present a speech.

33. I feel anxious while waiting to give my speech.

34. While giving a speech, I get so nervous I forget facts I really know.

Scoring: To determine your score on the PRPSA, complete the following steps:

Step 1. Add scores for items 1, 2, 3, 5, 9, 10, 13, 14, 19, 20, 21, 22, 23, 25, 27, 28, 29, 30, 31, 32, 33, and 34

Step 2. Add the scores for items 4, 6, 7, 8, 11, 12, 15, 16, 17, 18, 24, and 26

Step 3. Complete the following formula:

PRPSA = 72 - Total from Step 2 + Total from Step 1. Your score should be between 34 and 170. If your score is below 34 or above 170, you have made a mistake in computing the score. Mean = 114.6; SD = 17.2

My Score

    a. High level of public speaking anxiety = > 131

    b. Moderate level of public speaking anxiety = 98-131

    c. Low level of public speaking anxiety = < 98

Anxiety Level Tracker

Before   After

Take your anxiety level now and take the test again after you complete the final speech. Measure how much your anxiety changed.

1.3 Who's Afraid of Public Speaking?

Circle the following famous people expressed a deep fear of public speaking.

Adele	Aristotle	Rowan Atkinson	Warren Buffett	Winston Churchill
Leonardo DiCaprio	Harrison Ford	Sigmund Freud	Mahatma Gandhi	Rebecca Gibney
Hugh Grant	Samuel L. Jackson	Thomas Jefferson	Steve Jobs	Nicole Kidman
King George VI	Abraham Lincoln	Sir Isaac Newton	Joel Olstean	Anthony Quinn
Julia Roberts	Margaret Sanger	Jimmy Stewart	Barbara Streisand	Bruce Willis
Oprah Winfrey	Reese Witherspoon	Tiger Woods		

1.4 How Does Your Body React When You Stand in Front of an Audience to Speak?

Circle all that apply.

Physiological	Dry mouth	Enhanced sweat production
	Increased heart rate	Nausea
	Increased blood pressure	Stiffening of muscles
Non Verbal	Nervous shaking	Redundant behavior such as rocking back and forth, pacing, touching a part of the body repetitively, etc.
	Avoiding looking at the audience	
	Twisting legs	Blinking or *not* blinking (deer in the headlight look—eyes wide open)
Verbal	Stuttering	Using filler words including "like," "um," and "so," etc.
	Speaking too quickly	Inability to speak at all—freezing up
	Speaking too softly	

1.5 Is Your Life Limited by Fear, Dread or Phobia Associated with Speaking?

Does your unease regarding public speaking limit your life? If so, how?

If you could overcome or manage your fear, how would your life be different?

1.6 Filler Word Trivia

Filler Word Trivia: circle your favorite filler words.

Like	Right	Ah	I mean	Okay
Er	You know	So	Totally	Um

Who uses the most filler words? Check each that applies:

- ☐ Women
- ☐ Men
- ☐ Younger
- ☐ Older
- ☐ Disorganized Person
- ☐ Conscientious Person

Why do we insert filler words? Check each that applies:

- ☐ Stall for time
- ☐ Strengthen a statement
- ☐ Reduce harshness of statement
- ☐ Include listener
- ☐ Show you are thinking
- ☐ All of the above

1. **Know your audience** (Daly et. al, 1989).
2. **Know your room** (Daly et. al, 1989).
3. **Practice in front of people** (Smith & Frymeir, 2007).
4. **Practice** (Travis, 2004 & O'Hair et. al, 2001).
5. **Deliver speeches to audiences** (Smith & Frymeir, 2007).
6. **Share a personal story** (Widrich, Year & Hsu, 2008 & Stephens, Silbert & Hasson, 2010).
7. **Engage audience** (Steele, 2016).
8. **Clear purpose & points** (Steele, 2014 & Llopis, 2015).

1.7 Reduce Filler Words

Step 1: Choose one of these topics: aliens, Academy Awards, sports, self-driving cars, pets, Sunday afternoons, habits, rainy days, theater, college, stock market, politics, travel.

Step 2: Speak spontaneously for two minutes, delivering an impromptu speech using the word prompt you selected *without* using any filler words. Make every attempt to include the elements of a speech—an introduction, body and conclusion. Time yourself. Be sure you speak *without* using any filler words. The first time you use one, you are forgiven, the second time, your time is up! How long can you speak without using a filler word?

Record yourself speaking and listen for the patterns you use to "fill the space".

Note: This is a great activity to do with friends, even at a party; you can also do it alone by recording your speech. Repeat this activity as often as you like until you can reach the goal and control your use of filler words.

1.8 Losing Face

When was the last time you challenged someone's face?

When was the last time someone challenged your face?

Chapter 1 Review Questions

1. Describe the similarities between Dorothy and her friends facing the Great Oz and a person facing an audience.

2. Why do you believe people experience speech anxiety?

3. Describe some of the physical responses to speech anxiety. Do you exhibit any of these? Which ones?

4. What is the name of the phobia associated with the "fear of public speaking"?

5. How does the Yerkes-Dodson law apply to public speaking?

6. Describe a communication theory which explains why the fear/anxiety exists.

7. According to Stein, Walker and Forde, what is the least reason people fear public speaking and what is the main reaon? What is the difference between the two?

8. What are three typical responses to stress?

9. How does dread differ from fear?

10. Describe the difference between Stress and Anxiety.

11. What are three ways you can reduce anxiety?

12. How do we emotionally invest in our face?

13. Which quote from this chapter resonates with you the most?

Practice Speech: Story Time

Time Limit: 60-90 seconds or length of book.

Target Audience: Volunteer at the local library for a story hour with a group of twenty children, four to six years old. Assume that the reading area is located within a larger room, though separated somehow. You will need to speak loudly to keep the tykes' attention and everyone can hear you.

Instructions: Read a short, engaging child's book or story. Practice it a few times. Be sure that you rehearse enough to maintain eye contact 75% of the time. Speak with a relaxed throat and voice for natural projection. Use inflections to create excitement and enthusiasm. Use facial expressions to portray the story's emotions. Energize the story in every way you can, with vocal sounds and props if available.

Delivery Options

Option 1: Read the story to an imaginary audience in the largest room you can find. Use pillows or stuffed animals to substitute for the young tykes described in your target audience.

Option 2: Read the story to an imaginary audience in an outdoor open space like your backyard or a public park. Allow the plants and trees to substitute for the young tykes described in your target audience.

Option 3: Find some children who would enjoy listening to your story.

Option 4: Go to the library or local bookstore and actually read to a group of children.

Purpose: Ease yourself into the delivery process by providing a non-threatening venue. Focus on the variety of vocal inflections you use. Project your voice as much as you can. Create excitement by the energy you put into your voice.

Skills to practice: Breathe deeply. Explore your voice: your projection, your vocal inflection. Relax; get comfortable speaking in a non-threatening environment.

Resources: If you need a story, you may find a suitable one on this online list: http://www.magickeys. com/books/.

http://www.storylineonline.net is a website with an array of stories read by various authors. You can listen to the emphasis they put on words, the pace, and the emotion they add. If you worry about sounding monotone or boring, listen to the reader read one page, turn down the volume, and follow their example of emphasis as you read the page.

Sample Speech: The Boy Who Cried Wolf!

Author: Aesop's Fables

Note: You can read the entire background or just introduce and share the author.

Background: Aesop was reportedly a slave and storyteller who lived in Ancient Greece between 620 and 564 BC. Aristotle, Herodotus, and Plutarch all referenced Aesop and his fables, but no written stories penned by him have been found. At least six Greek and Latin authors captured the stories on paper, but their writings were lost over time. Even so, over the past 2,500 years, his words have not only survived, but also travelled around the globe. They have been modified and repeatedly shared in many forms, from sermons to children's stories. Due to constant revision and interpretation, today's body of fables attributed to Aesop bears little relation to those he originally told. The first English version of Aesop's Fables was printed in 1484 by William Caxton (Keller, J. E., & Keating, L. C. (1993), and even those have evolved.

The Boy Who Cried Wolf

There once was a shepherd boy who was bored as he sat on the hillside watching the village sheep. To amuse himself he took a great breath and sang out, "Wolf! Wolf! The Wolf is chasing the sheep!"

The villagers came running up the hill to help the boy drive the wolf away. But when they arrived at the top of the hill, they found no wolf. The boy laughed at the sight of their angry faces.

"Don't cry 'wolf', shepherd boy," said the villagers, "when there's no wolf!" They went grumbling back down the hill.

Later, the boy sang out again, "Wolf! Wolf! The wolf is chasing the sheep!" To his naughty delight, he watched the villagers run up the hill to help him drive the wolf away.

When the villagers saw no wolf, they sternly said, "Save your frightened song for when there is really something wrong! Don't cry 'wolf' when there is *no* wolf!"

But the boy just grinned and watched them go grumbling down the hill once more.

Later, he saw a **real** wolf prowling about his flock. Alarmed, he leapt to his feet and sang out as loudly as he could, "Wolf! Wolf!"

But the villagers thought he was trying to fool them again, and so they didn't come.

At sunset, everyone wondered why the shepherd boy hadn't returned to the village with their sheep. They went up the hill to find the boy. They found him weeping.

"There really was a wolf here! The flock has scattered! I cried out, "Wolf!" Why didn't you come?"

An old man tried to comfort the boy as they walked back to the village.

"We'll help you look for the lost sheep in the morning," he said, putting his arm around the youth, "Nobody believes a liar . . . even when he is telling the truth!"

Practice Speech: Poem Out Loud

Time Limit: 60 seconds

Target Audience: Envision reading an inspiring poem to a group of 75 guests honoring a mentor or a positive influence in your life (a parent, teacher, or boss) for their service to a non-profit organization like Kids in Distress or the American Cancer Society. You have the opportunity to convey your feelings about your mentor by reading this poem.

Instructions: Read a short poem that you find meaningful. Be sure that you rehearse enough to maintain eye contact 75% of the time. Decide on the type of feeling you want to convey to your audience. Is this a happy poem to make people smile? Or is this a poem to be taken more seriously? Each type of poem demands a different tone of voice and pace of words. If available, listen to an online reading of the poem and incorporate vocal inflection in your own reading. Then practice conveying the concepts, theme, and feeling of the poem through your voice.

Delivery Options

Option 1: Read the poem to an imaginary audience in your living room. Stand tall in front of the pillows on your couch for they will act as your audience.

Option 2: When you see a group of people on TV, pause the scene and practice giving your speech to them. Stand tall. Look them in the eye when giving your speech.

Option 3: Read your poem aloud to someone you trust. It can just be one person. Stand tall and establish eye contact. Be sure to create the tone you want.

Purpose: Get comfortable projecting your voice with different emotions and vocal inflections. Notice how your body, facial expressions, hand gestures physically react to the emotion and emphasis you add to the various lines.

Skills to practice: Project your voice; add emotion, inflection, and energy. Relax and deliver a reading in a non-threatening environment.

Resources:

Here is a website of 500 famous poems. You can select one that speaks to you!
https://allpoetry.com/classics/famous_poems

Both of these resource have many poems to choose from, but they also provide resources to listen to poetry and tips on reciting. Listen to the inflection in the reader's voice and try to mimic strategies you hear. This will help you learn to use more inflection in your voice.

http://www.poetryoutloud.org/poems-and-performance/find-poems
https://www.poetryfoundation.org/poems-and-poets/poems

Sample Poem: The Road Not Taken by Robert Frost

Context: Robert Frost was one of the most popular American poets. He was born 1874 and died in 1963. Like "The Road Not Taken," published in 1916, Frost's poems often feature the New England countryside. This poem may be his most frequently cited work.

Two roads diverged in a yellow wood,
And sorry I could not travel both
And be one traveler, long I stood
And looked down one as far as I could
To where it bent in the undergrowth;

Then took the other, as just as fair,
And having perhaps the better claim,
Because it was grassy and wanted wear;
Though as for that the passing there
Had worn them really about the same,

And both that morning equally lay
In leaves no step had trodden black.
Oh, I kept the first for another day!
Yet knowing how way leads on to way,
I doubted if I should ever come back.

I shall be telling this with a sigh
Somewhere ages and ages hence:
Two roads diverged in a wood, and I—
I took the one less traveled by,
And that has made all the difference.

Note: After you have read it with meaning, it might be fun to listen to actual professional readings of the poem located on YouTube.

Everything you want is on the other side of fear.
– George Adair

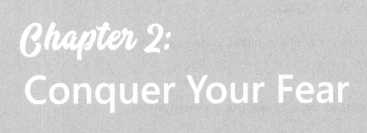

Chapter 2:
Conquer Your Fear

Objectives

By the end of this chapter you should be able to:

1. Explain why popular myths about public speaking can harm one's delivery.

2. Identify anxiety-reducing tips.

3. Establish a deliberate practice that incorporates the 5 Speech Delivery Tactics.

4. Discover the secret to overcoming your fear of public speaking.

5. Believe you can transform your ability to communicate.

2.1 Myth or Fact

Often these "simple" suggestions can actually thwart your ability to connect with your audience and even interfere with the speech.

Mark each box: 'T' for **True** if you think the myth has merit, and 'F' for **False** if you think it doesn't.

☐   Imagine the audience naked or in their underwear.

☐   Avoid eye contact—focus at a point above the audiences heads.

☐   Begin with a joke.

☐   Too much rehearsal is bad for me—I'm better just speaking off the cuff.

☐   Just go straight for the Q & A.

☐   You are born with the talent of public speaking—you cannot learn it.

☐   Memorize your speech.

☐   Shut off the lights to show an electronic presentation.

☐   Being a good public speaker involves eliminating nervousness.

☐   A mistake will destroy the speech.

☐   Hide behind the podium.

☐   My experience trumps credible sources.

2.2 Which of These Five Tips Will Be Most Beneficial to You?

Number these five techniques from **most** beneficial to **least**.

_____ Imagine Yourself Nailing the Speech!

_____ Use Your Breath to Control Your Nerves

_____ Think Positively

_____ Practice Power Poses

_____ Dress Professionally

Take Action Now!: Take out your smart phone if you have one, go to your clock and create a reminder to repeat these words at an ideal time every day until your speech is due: "My audience will LOVE my speech." After you say these words, close your eyes and imagine their faces completely appreciating every word you say.

2.3 Quality Practice

Researchers studied each of the items listed below to identify which could predict the best speech performance. Check each one that you think proved to work.

_____ cue cards _____ visual aids _____ state anxiety

_____ silent rehearsal _____ total preparation time _____ oral rehearsal

_____ other research _____ grade point average _____ number of rehearsals for an audience

How to Establish a Deliberate Practice

1. Set an intentional "stretch" goal. Which means, to target a specific area in which you want to improve. Identify measurable improvement points along the way. Each time you practice, "stretch" yourself to reach that next point. Be sure that your practice supports your efforts to improve to that point. Evaluate your progress.
2. Focus 100%! Eliminate any distractions. It is necessary to hit a deep level of focus. This is a huge challenge in today's society with the constant interruptions of our cell phones and social media.
3. Get feedback! The feedback should be immediate and of high quality. Top athletes or performers get feedback that occurs on the spot. The feedback needs to be from qualified experts.
4. Reflect and refine. Duckworth explains that this step is the hardest. You must have the courage to receive feedback without being defensive.

Chapter 2 Review Questions

1. Prior to reading the chapter, did you believe any of the myths? Which one? Explain why it is a myth.

2. Identify a new tip you offer to a developing speaker.

3. Practice one of the paractice speeches being sure to follow the Five Steps to Practice a Speech, write a one paragraph analysis of the experience.

4. Have you ever followed Duckworth's guidelines to establish a deliberate practice? Explain. Identify a time in your life when you practiced poorly. What did you do differently? How did it impact your performance? Is it better to practice with intent?

5. What is the "ultimate secret" to overcoming your fear of public speaking?

6. What are some tips for reducing anxiety?

7. List the steps for establishing a deliberate practice.

8. What are the five steps to practicing a speech?

9. Identify atleast three public speaking tactics or myths that have been debunked. Explain why these are no longer the case.

10. Why is it critical to breathe properly during a speech?

11. Why is dressing professionally for a speech important? Provide one example for male and female of what's considered appropriate.

12. What does the concept of being "speech actualized" mean?

13. In the model of communication presented what are the three components featured? Which should be the most important during a speech?

14. Which quote from this chapter resonates with you the most?

Practice Speech: Amaze and Astound Your Favorite Animal

Time Limit: 60 seconds

Target Audience: Deliver these heart warming quotes about animals to an animal; either a cat, dog, bird or fish—you can even choose an animal at the zoo should you be inspired.

Instructions: Select your favorite five quotes from the great animal quotes listed after these instructions. Implement your best practice techniques. Establish a deliberate practice using Duckworth's steps.

1. Determine your stretch goal. For each quote, apply one suggestion from each list.

Delivery Tips & Techniques	Anxiety Reducing Strategies
Familiarize yourself with the words of the speech	Imagine yourself nailing the speech
Choose the right inflection and emotion	Use your breath to control your nerves.
Identify key words you will emphasize	Think positively
Focus on the beginning of your speech	Practice power poses
Practice in front of an audience.	Dress professionally

2. Focus 100%—no outside interruptions!

3. Use feedback! Were you aware of attention from your audience? Record yourself and ask for feedback from someone you trust.

4. Reflect and refine!

Purpose: Establish a deliberate practice. Implement anxiety-reducing strategies with a non-threatening audience. Explore the array of available options to make your words interesting and compelling. Get comfortable standing in front of an audience who you know won't judge you! As you approach this speech, be aware of your nerves and fear, then remember that your audience is an animal. This should relieve your fear and help you deliver your speech boldly, with emotion, incorporating the strategies above. Always consider your audience.

Skills to practice:

*   Establish a deliberate practice.
*   Project your voice, add emotion, in inflection and energy.
*   Relax . . . deliver a reading in a non-threatening environment.

Sample Animal Quotes

"Animals are such agreeable friends—they ask no questions, they pass no criticisms."
—George Eliot

"Until one has loved an animal, a part of one's soul remains un-awakened." — Anatole France

"If having a soul means being able to feel love and loyalty and gratitude, then animals are better off than a lot of humans."— James Herriot

"The animals of the world exist for their own reasons. They were not made for humans any more than black people were made for white, or women created for men." — Alice Walker

"Happiness is a warm puppy." — Charles M. Schulz

"The greatness of a nation and its moral progress can be judged by the way its animals are treated." — Mahatma Gandhi

"An animal's eyes have the power to speak a great language." — Martin Buber

"Man is the cruelest animal." — Friedrich Nietzsche

"Meow" means "woof" in cat." — George Carlin

"If you pick up a starving dog and make him prosperous he will not bite you. This is the principal difference between a dog and man." — Mark Twain

"How it is that animals understand things I do not know, but it is certain that they do understand. Perhaps there is a language which is not made of words and everything in the world understands it. Perhaps there is a soul hidden in everything and it can always speak, without even making a sound, to another soul." — Frances Hodgson Burnett

"Clearly, animals know more than we think, and think a great deal more than we know."
— Irene M. Pepperberg

"A dog is the only thing on earth that loves you more than he loves himself." — Josh Billings

"If a dog will not come to you after having looked you in the face, you should go home and examine your conscience." — Woodrow Wilson

"Animals are born who they are, accept it, and that is that. They live with greater peace than people do." — Gregory Maguire

"I am fond of pigs. Dogs look up to us. Cats look down on us. Pigs treat us as equals."
— Winston S. Churchill

"Heaven goes by favor. If it went by merit, you would stay out and your dog would go in."
— Mark Twain

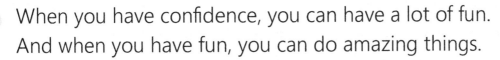

> When you have confidence, you can have a lot of fun.
> And when you have fun, you can do amazing things.
>
> *– Joe Namath*

Chapter 3:
Transform Your Delivery

Objectives

By the end of this chapter you should be able to:

1. Recall key terminology necessary to critique a speech.

2. Detect behaviors speakers use to create interest and evoke an audience.

3. Spot speaker behaviors which cause audience members to typically disengage or respond negatively.

4. Discover the Ten Delivery Principles.

5. Examine which delivery principles you will find to be most challenging.

6. Master Delivery Principle 1-6 using the Practice Speeches.

3.1 Behaviors of Great Speakers

Put a checkmark next to each behavior great speakers exhibit and an 'X' next to behaviors great speakers never do.

_____ Great pace, not too slow, not too fast

_____ Aware of audience verbal or nonverbal cues

_____ Responded to audience verbal or nonverbal cues

_____ Considered perspective of individual audience members

_____ Accurately anticipated audience response to the message

_____ Balanced information with explanation

_____ Told stories

_____ Got you to think about your stories

_____ Creatively involved audience

_____ Used visuals or props that helped information take form and meaning

_____ Creatively incorporated visuals and/or props by engaging audience

_____ Carefully considered what to do and how to do it so

_____ Rewarded audience members for response

_____ Expressed gratitude for audience's undivided attention

_____ Spoke fast, difficult to grasp information or spoke slow, frustrating to follow

_____ Unaware of audience verbal or nonverbal cues

_____ Did not respond to audience verbal or nonverbal cues

_____ Made blanket generalization about groups and/or sub groups

_____ Poorly anticipated audience response to the message

_____ All information without explanation

_____ No personal stories told, stuck to the facts.

_____ Did not ask audience members questions

_____ Spoke to the audience but failed to involve them

_____ Visuals or props distracted from information or

_____ Poorly incorporated visuals or props

_____ Shared the content without evidence of careful thought or consideration

_____ Sat down and received applause

3.2 Use the Right Word to Rate the Speaker

Step 1: Familiarize yourself with these words.

Step 2: Listen to a TED Talk at www.TED.com

Step 3: Score the speaker on a scale of 1-5 on how well they illustrated each of these words in their speech. Mark the number on the left space of the Score on the Vocabulary Words.

Step 4: Self Analysis. Consider your capacity as a speaker. Using the scoring provided on a scale of 1-5, how would you rate your ability to do each of these well in a speech. Redeliver one of the speeches you have delivered for the first two chapters or evaluate your use of the vocabulary words when you complete the practice speeches at the end of this chapter. Score yourself on the right slot next to each word. On a scale of 1-5, rate your ability to fully realize the opportunity each word offers to enhance your speaking ability. Periodically reevaluate yourself and assess your progress.

Developing Your Public Speaking Vocabulary

Read the definitions of these words. Listen to someone deliver a speech. See if you can determine how well the speaker fared on these different ideas. Compare several different speakers, even those on TV. What do you like? What do you not like? What did the speaker do well? Once you have analyzed others, put yourself on stage!

Determine how well you score in each area. Consider those areas you need improvement. Incorporate in your Delivery Action Plan. When possible, present a speech in front of an audience. Actively solicit their feedback; determine if they score your performance the same way.

Verbal Elements	Definition	Score 1-5	
		self	speaker
Articulation	Speak clearly, distinctly		
Cadence	Rhythmic sequence or flow of sounds in language		
Emphasis	Intensity, significance or stress that gives impressiveness or importance to something		
Enunciation	Pronounce all syllables clearly		
Language	Specific word choice used		
Inflection	Change in pitch or loudness of voice; the change of form that words undergo to mark such distinctions as those of case, gender, number, tense, person, mood, or voice.		
Pace	Rate of performance or delivery: Tempo		
Pitch	Difference in the relative vibration frequency of the human voice that contributes to the total meaning of speech		
Projection	Control of the volume, clarity, and distinctness of a voice to gain greater audibility		
Pronunciation	Articulating a sound or word		
Volume	Degree of loudness or intensity of a sound		
Wording	Act or manner of expressing with words, words selected to express a thought		

Non-Verbal Elements	Definition	Score 1-5	
		self	speaker
Audience connection	Degree to which you cause your audience to focus on your message; created by a combination of mannerisms, poise, leadership, enthusiasm, food, visuals, voice, projection, etc.		

Aura	Distinctive atmosphere surrounding a given source
Body Language	Bodily mannerisms, postures, & facial expressions that can be interpreted as unconsciously communicating a person's feelings or psychological state
Commitment	Loyalty, devotion or dedication
Confidence	Feeling or consciousness of one's powers or of reliance on one's circumstance; faith or belief that one will act in a right, proper, or effective way
Contextual Background	Parts of a written or spoken statement that precede or follow a specific word or passage, usually influencing its meaning or effect, set of circumstances or facts that surround a particular event. The social, historical, and other antecedents or causes of an event or condition
Dress	Choice of clothing
Dynamic	Relating to energy; marked by usually continuous and productive activity or change
Energy	Vigor, liveliness and forcefulness. The capacity of a body or system to do work
Eye Contact	Act of looking directly into the eyes of another person
Facial Expressions	Communicates information about emotions
Gestures	Form of nonverbal communication in which visible bodily actions are used to communicate particular messages, either in place of speech or together and in parallel with spoken words
Manage your "Face" (Face work)	If challenged by your audience, avoid engaging in a tit-for-tat exchange save face by recognizing the challenger and redirecting the focus of the speech in the direction you want. When challenged by one's audience, always handle your response politely & never give away your power as the speaker. (You exemplify leadership for the audience.)
Pause	Brief suspension of the voice to indicate the limits and relations of sentences and their part; a reason or cause for pausing (as to reconsider)
Poise	A well-balanced state; easy self-possessed assurance of manner; gracious tact in coping or handling
Posture	Way in which someone carries his or her body; body position or bearing
Practice	Activities involved in preparing for a presentation, considering not just words but additional elements such as handouts, visuals and other elements. Ready and able to deal with something
Proxemics	Space dynamics. Study of how we perceive and use intimate, personal, social, and public space in various settings including awareness and dictates of cultural paradigms
Tone	Used to set the mood; any sound considered with reference to its quality, pitch, strength, source, etc.; quality or character of sound; a particular style or manner, as of writing or speech

Ten Delivery Principles Every Speaker Should Use

DP1 *Set the Stage*

Start smart. Begin your speech with caution and care consciously aware of the factors that create the audience's first impression. Your speech begins well before you ever open your mouth. Consider each stage and how they impact your speech.

- **Before the speech:** Includes your attitude about delivery, degree of preparation, your confidence level and various non verbal messages.
- **Taking the stage:** Includes how organized you appear, your stride, posture and confidence level, and even how friendly and approachable you appear.
- **Establish:** Stand before audience feet firmly planted, exude friendly confidence through posture and poise, establish rapport through eye contact and calmly wait each and every audience member to "be ready" to hear your words.
- **First spoken words:** Know your first two lines. Project the words using plenty of vocal variety and pauses for impact. (Be careful to not look down at your cards and break the connection with the audience.)

DP2 *Control the Energy*

Beware and aware of the competing energies in any given speaking environment. Speaker's energy, audience energy and room dynamics each intersect to create a given dynamic. Anticipate and respond appropriately to create a conducive, receptive environment.

- **Speaker's Energy:** Speaker energy related to and about the presentation (are you excited or dreading, prepared or unprepared) and your energy outside the presentation (your health or stressors that impact your personal energy).
- **Audience's Energy:** Collective energy of the group (high/low, weak/strong) vs individual group member's energy (negative/positive).
- **Room Energy:** The size, temperature, lighting and set up all influence the feeling of the presentation.

DP3 *Speak Up!*

Engage your diaphragm to speak up. Speaking from your diaphragm ensures that your words resonate from deep within you and are fueled by your breath. Speaking from your throat rather than your diaphragm over time can damage your vocal cords. There is a direct correlation between controlling nervous energy and speaking up. The more you speak up confidently, the more control you will exert over anxiety.

DP4 *Sweeten It!*

Make the speech all that it can be by taking advantage of every opportunity your speech allows. Each speech contains specific opportunities to consciously engage the audience and make the content come alive. Consider how you can capitalize on every opportunity. Consider incorporating each of the five senses; implement each delivery principle to the best of your ability. Most people have few opportunities to stand before an audience and create change...make the most of the opportunity, make the speech all that it can be.

DP5 *Power of the Pause*

Powerful use of silence to solicit a specific response from the audience. Four types of pauses are: transitional, dramatic, impact, unplanned. Often, pauses should be planned prior to delivery.

1. **Transitional:** Pause used to notify the audience of a change in ideas both large (points) and small (research and connections). Length of the pause depends upon the size of the change.
2. **Dramatic:** Pause used to add impact to an idea. Can be used to gain attention usually for humor or to make a profound point, like asking probing questions of the audience.
3. **Impact:** A short pause used to create emphasis and interest prior to verbally emphasizing certain words with tone and pitch. Typically incorporated prior to numbers, conjunctions, adjectives and pronouns a short pause is inserted before the verbal emphasis is added.
4. **Unplanned:** Strategy a speaker incorporates live to reset the focus or direction of the speech. Speaker stops speaking and waits long enough to continue the speech as planned.
   - Audience Regroup: Audience attention wanes or gets off topic responding to a disruption.
   - Speaker Regroup: Speaker may get off topic or competing thoughts make it difficult to formulate cohesive sentences.
   - Sentence Regroup: Strategy to pause long enough to identify the right word rather than insert filler words.

DP6 *Engage, Engage, Engage*

Planned, thoughtful ways to keep your audience involved in your presentation. The 4 Ps for an engaging speech include:

1. **Personal stories:** Share personal stories that includes details: who, what, where, why, how and how. Don't be afraid to be vulnerable.
2. **Probing questions:** Ask probing questions that require the audience to conjure up their own experience and connection to the content.
3. **Props (3D):** Incorporate objects that demonstrate or illustrate content from your speech. Be creative.
4. **Physical activities:** Inject activities that require at least two audience members to move from sitting in their seat. (Stand request to verify audience response/role plays).

DP7 *Use Your Space Wisely*

Consider your use of space and how you can use your space to solicit the best audience response. Cultural influences create a powerful response to space dynamics within each of us. Breaking cultural norms can be a very powerful way to gain the audience's attention. Your space includes various different elements.

- **Stage:** The stage itself can differ greatly varying from a formal lifted stage placing you above your audience to a less formal space in front of an audience. In either situation always strive to get as close to your audience as possible. Either bring yourself to the audience or bring members of the audience to you physically or verbally by identifying specific audience members or targeting areas in the audience i.e. those of you in the back row.
- **Podium or Lectern:** A podium is a raised platform and a lectern is a slanted high desk often used to place speaking notes during a lecture. Often one or the other will be provided for your use as a speaker. Just because it is there does not mean that you are required to use it or are tied to it. The situation often dictates which rules to follow. Consider whether or not you can step out from behind the podium or if the situation is formal and requires you to adhere to the spot behind the podium. Whenever you have the opportunity to shrug the podium or lectern do so as you can incorporate body language and movement and get closer to your audience.
- **Audience:** Just because you as the speaker are given a space in front of the audience, doesn't mean you can't break free from the confines of the stage and go into the audience or incorporate other areas in the room into your speech. Move audience members, incorporate "plants" in your audience to toy with the proxemics of the group.
- **Body Language:** Never show your audience your backside. Keep your body open to your audience. You can validate that your body is open to your audience by extending your arms directly out from the angle of your shoulders—is your audience included in the embrace? At any given point and time during the speech, your arms should be able to embrace your audience, if they can't move your body. No matter where you are, left, right or center, your upper torso and shoulders should be directed towards your audience, never away from them.

DP8 *Respect*

Respect the time, premise for the event and the cultural influences at stake. Speaking engagements fit into events in a very specific way. First and foremost respect the guidelines and have an awareness of where the presentation fits into the event. Depending upon the location and cultural nuances at play, you as the speaker should adapt to the specific contexts of the engagement.

DP9 *Dance with Your Audience*

Acute awareness of how each audience member responds to each word, pause and gesture you convey and your ability to read and respond appropriately to fulfill the ultimate purpose for the speech.

DP10 *Have Fun!*

Ability to be "in the moment" able to enjoy and actually have fun with the experience, executing each delivery principle effortlessly. Point where you are able to empower your words using the energy the anxiety creates to deliver your best speech.

- Master implementing all the delivery principles.
- Feel the excitement you have for the well planned out activities
- Appreciate the audience's response to you and
- Relax in the knowledge that you have worked hard and are confident in your ability to connect and share a message that matters with your audience.

3.3 Breakdown of Set the Stage

Create a checklist of things you must do to master setting the stage.

Before	Taking the Stage	Establish	First Word

3.4 Toy with Your Energy (Control Your Energy)

Stand up with your feet shoulder width apart. Hold your arms out with your palms facing each other. Take a deep breath. Slowly let it out. Close your eyes and slowly, very slowly, bring your palms together. As you move your hands toward each other, concentrate on what you feel. Do you feel a slight resistance? Maybe the inside of your palms are slightly warm? How about a little tingly feeling? As your palms move closer, the resistance might increase. Play with it; see if you can mold it into an energy ball. Continue to push your palms together and actually push the energy into yourself.

What you've just experienced is your personal energy; the energy surging through your body that keeps all of us alive. This energy is your life force.

3.5 Speaking from Fear or Confidence (Speak Up)

Try doing this physically.

Version 1: Adopt a posture that projects fear. What happens to your body? Do your shoulders slouch and head move forward and down? In this position, say "This will be my best speech ever."

Version 2: Now adopt a posture that projects pride and confidence. Remember Amy Cuddy's Power Poses we discussed in Chapter 1? Stand like Wonder Woman or Superman! Can you feel your shoulders move back, head up? Now say, "This will be my best speech ever."

Question:
1. Which version did you Speak Up more?
2. Which version did you believe more?

Isn't it amazing how a change in our posture can project a completely different emotion from us? Besides adopting "power poses" how does one project their voice? In order for you to increase your volume, you must exert more energy to do so. Focus on this relationship between your volume level and the energy you exert to speak. Raise your energy level and your projection naturally follows (unless you are intentionally trying to whisper). Connecting with your diaphragm and learning to breath deeply, will help you use your breath to empower your words.

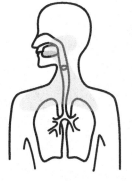 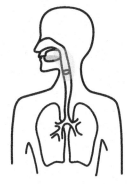

Speaking from the diaphragm
sound areas: upper chest, vocal chords, and back of mouth

Speaking from the throat
sound areas: throat and upper neck

3.6 Name That Tune (Sweeten It!)

Name a song you think would be known and liked by everyone, from 9-99 years old.

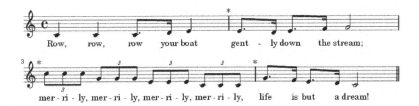

Row, row, row your boat gent - ly down the stream; mer - ri - ly, mer - ri - ly, mer - ri - ly, mer - ri - ly, life is but a dream!

3.7 Ways to Sweeten It

1. Think of the speeches you have heard. What is the best example of one where the speaker creatively, made the speech *all* that it could be?

2. What did they do to "sweeten it"?

3. Imagine you are delivering the following speeches, what could you do sweeten the speech and incorporate several senses?
   a. Introduction speech for Willy Wonka.

   b. Speech about why marriages fail.

   c. Speech about how to paddle board.

   d. Safety speech about how to respond in a crisis to a hurricane.

4. Perhaps you've thought of ideas like these:
   a. Sound & Sight: Song Pure Imagination from Movie, Taste & touch: Willy Wonka candy with a golden ticket.
   b. Touch/Sound/Sight Role Play: Two participants act out marriage vows, while wedding music plays. Taste & smell wedding cake.
   c. Sound/Song Surfin' Safari, Touch/sight: Paddle board, life vest, paddle. Taste/smell tropical juice drink or pineapple.
   d. Sound: Emergency broadcast system. Touch/Smell/Sight 72 hour survival kit (include treats) flash light, radio.

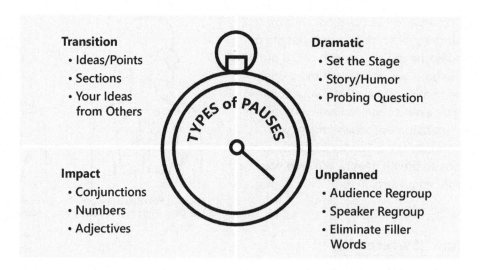

3.8 Entitle Pausing for Pauses (Power of the Pause)

Review two minutes of a speech. Count the pauses and identify the type of pause used for each.

1. Transitional	2. Dramatic	3. Impact	4. Unplanned

3.9 Which Speech is Better? (Engage, Engage, Engage)

Suppose you are delivering a basic speech introducing yourself. This group meets to advance your interest in your hobby—like photography or sailing or even Toastmasters. Do a short speech of introduction about yourself.

Version 1: A straightforward speech responding to the questions listed.

1. State your name.
2. Describe who you are – where you are from, cultural background, current role or place within an organization.
3. Provide a background – how did you come to be a part of this group? Why?
4. What is the most interesting thing about you? What is your primary interest, goal or particular passion – especially as it relates to this group.
5. Is there anything the group should know about you? Great talent, hobby, accomplishment or pet peeve?
6. What do you hope to gain from the group? Why?

Version 2: Engages your audience using each of the 4 Ps.

Personal Story:	Probe:	Physical:	Prop:

Which Speech is better? Version 1: No Engagement or version 2: Engaged Speech

Decode the graph

In this example, the graph speaks volumes of what happened in the speech.

0:10 Asked a probing question.

1:20 Speaker lost their place, got flustered but regrouped (that's the huge drop).

2:30 Prop to illustrate a point.

3:50 Told a story.

4:30 Got off topic and just started going in circles.

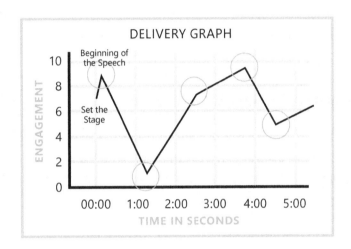

3.10 Space Dynamics (Use Your Space Wisely)

Consider the last presentation you heard, what might the speaker have done to further engage the audience by considering his or her use of space.

Proxemics

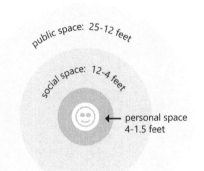

Relative Distance Between People (Hall, 1976, p.41)

Public space	12 to 25 feet range	The distance maintained between an audience and a speaker (in a formal setting).
Social space	4 to 12 feet range	Used for communication among business associates, as well as to separate strangers using public areas, such as beaches and bus stops.
Personal space	18 inches to 4 feet	Used among friends and family members. Another example would be between people waiting in lines.
Intimate space	out to 18 inches	Involves a high probability of touching. We reserve it for whispering and embracing.

Note: These rules differ by culture.

29

3.11 Check Your Time (Respect the Time)

1. What cultural perspective do you have on time?

2. If you are invited to a party, what time do you arrive?

3. Does the organization where the speech is being given adhere to M (monochromic) or P (polychromic) time?

3.12 Engage or Dance? (Dance with Your Audience)

1. Dancing with the Audience: Think of a time when you were in an audience with a speaker who danced with you. How did that feel? How did it work?

2. Describe a time when a speaker engaged you as an audience member. What action did they take to create the engagement?

3. What is the difference between dancing with your audience and engaging them?

Chapter 3 Review Questions

1. Without looking, list as many words as you can that relate to public speaking.

2. Describe speaker behaviors that can cause the audience to disengage and speaker behaviors that cause the audience to engage.

2. List the 10 Delivery Principles.

    1.

    2.

    3.

    4.

    5.

    6.

    7.

    8.

    9.

    10.

4. What are the four different stages you need to consider before you begin a speech? What are the three types of energy to consider?

5. Which four words should always have a pause and vocal variety added?

6. What does the respect principle refer to exactly?

7. What must you do prior to attempting DP10: Have Fun?

8. Which delivery principle do you think will be the easiest for you to master? Why? Which will be the most difficult? Why?

9. Which quote from this chapter resonates with you the most?

Practice Speech: Famous

Time Limit: 90 seconds

Target Audience: Given your desire to develop your public speaking skills, you decide to compete in the Speeches from History competition at the County Fair. The audience ranges from old folks to kids, family to strangers, and the judges. It is set in an outdoor arena where the horses were shown earlier in the day. You do have a microphone, but face competition from noise in other parts of the fair.

Instructions: History is filled with moments when someone has formulated and presented a speech worthy of recognition.

- Locate a 45 second excerpt (three to five sentences only) from a fantastic speech in history— words that influenced others. Make sure the topic matters to both you and your audience.
- Provide a context for the speech, explaining why you chose that specific one and why it's relevant to your audience. You can begin with the speech itself or an introduction explaining why you chose it. If you use an introduction, keep it less than half the length of the original text.
- Practice deliberately incorporating the 5 Tactics for Practicing a Speech.
- Record yourself delivering the speech.
- Reflect on your delivery, identifying your strengths and weaknesses. Open yourself to the process of improving your ability to communicate.

Purpose:

1. Incorporate the "Ultimate Secret" in overcoming your speech anxiety. Consider your audience needs more than your own.

2. Deliver iconic powerful words that changed lives. Appreciate their worth. Consider the historical significance lying behind those words. Harness this awareness to empower your voice.

3. Establish a Deliberate Practice focusing on the first three Delivery Principles. Make it your stretch goal to master DP1: Set the Stage. Mastery of DP1 involves effectively using DP2: Control the Energy, and DP3: Speak Up.

4. Record yourself delivering the speech.

5. Reflect on your delivery, identifying your strengths and weaknesses. Open yourself to the process of improving your ability to communicate.

Skills to Practice: Ultimate Secret to Overcoming Your Fear. DP1: Set the Stage, DP2: Control the Energy, DP3: Speak Up.

Resources:

- History Channel: http://www.history.com/speeches
- History Place: http://www.historyplace.com/speeches/previous.htm
- American Rhetoric: http://www.americanrhetoric.com/speechbank.htm
- Gifts of Speech: http://gos.sbc.edu

Sample Speech: "To Be Fed" originally delivered by Oprah Winfrey

Interpreted by Alexis Kent

Context: When Alexis Kent submitted this speech for her Famous Speech assignment, she did the assignment perfectly. She found a speech that spoke to her and proceeded to plug into the needs of her audience. How did she make this happen? She asked a few pertinent questions to get the audience on board—pay attention to the ones she chose for the beginning of the speech. While there are more "iconic" famous speeches, Alexis makes her selection relevant to the audience by providing a meaningful context. Be sure you do likewise. This personifies the Ultimate Secret in overcoming your speech anxiety: thinking more about the audience's needs than your own.

Introduction: Think about this, coming into this class for the first time and introducing yourself to everyone sitting in the audience. How many of you were concerned about the first impression you made? What they would think about you? People, by nature, want to feel **accepted** by everyone because, well, how many people really want to be **disliked**? **Oprah Winfrey** delivered this speech after receiving the first **Bob Hope Humanitarian Award** at the **Emmy Awards** on September 22, 2002. I located this speech on Alchin's (2011) database of speeches. This is what Oprah said about the **homeless** people her father brought to family gatherings:

Speech Excerpt: And I would often say to my father afterwards, 'Dad, why can't we just have **regular** people at our **Christmas** dinner?' ... And my father said to me, 'They are regular people. They're just like you. They want the same thing you want.' And I would say, 'What?' And he'd say, '**To be fed.**' And at the time, I just thought he was talking about dinner. But I have since learned how **profound** he really was... we all just want to know that **we matter**. We want **validation**. We want the **same things**. We want **safety** and we want to **live** a long life. We want to **find somebody to love**... We want to find somebody to **laugh with** and have the **power** and the **place to cry** with when **necessary**.

Conclusion: This speech resonates with me because I, just like everyone in this room, want to find that person to **share everything with**. So, just think before you **judge** a book by its **cover**. "**We all just want to be fed.**"

References: Alchin, L. (2011, February 16). Oprah Winfrey speech: 54th Emmy awards. Retrieved from http://www.famous-speeches-and-speech-topics.info/famous-speeches-by-women/oprah-winfrey-speech.htm

Note: The bold words were selected by the speaker for emphasis.

Practice Speech: Movie

Time Limit: 60–90 seconds

Instructions: What is your favorite speech from a movie? The golden screen has a way of capturing some incredible speeches that deeply move us. Locate a short excerpt of a monologue or speech from a movie that stands out to you. Loosen up and deliver the speech with the same energy and passion as the speaker from the movie. Relax and have fun!

Target Audience: Adopt the audience from the movie scene you select.

Purpose:

1. Deliver iconic powerful words captured on screen. Appreciate their worth. Use the preselected words to empower your voice.

2. Focus on the first three Delivery Principles. Make it your goal to master DP1: Set the Stage. Since DPI, DP2 and DP3 are inherently intertwined, mastering DP1 will also satisfy the requirement for mastering DP2: Speak Up, and DP3: Assess and Cope.

3. Record yourself delivering the speech.

4. Reflect on your delivery, identifying your strengths and weaknesses. Open yourself to the process of improving your ability to communicate.

Skills to Practice: Continue to focus on mastery of DP1: Set the Stage, DP2: Control the Energy, DP3: Speak Up. Use your body to communicate your message—facial expressions, hand gestures and movement.

Resources:

American Rhetoric: http://www.americanrhetoric.com/moviespeeches.htm

Film Site offers a database of over 700 of the Best Film Speeches and Monologues. http://www.filmsite.org/bestspeeches.html

Sample Movie: *Remember the Titans* (2000)

Coach Herman Boone: Gettysburg Speech

Background: *Remember the Titans* is set during the time of segregation; an all white and all black school are closed down forcing the two schools to become T.C. Williams High School. At the start of football season the head coach, Coach Boone, takes the players on a trip to Gettysburg so they will learn to trust each other and get along. Coach Boone wakes the players and other coaches at 3:00 in the morning and runs the team several miles to the site of Gettysburg. These are the words he speaks to inspire his team.

Speech Excerpt: Anybody know what this place is? This is Gettysburg. This is where they fought the Battle of Gettysburg. Fifty thousand men died right here on this field, fightin' the same fight that we're still fightin' amongst ourselves today.

This green field right here was painted red, bubblin' with the blood of young boys, smoke and hot lead pourin' right through their bodies. Listen to their souls, men:

'I killed my brother with malice in my heart. Hatred destroyed my family.'

You listen. And you take a lesson from the dead. If we don't come together, right now, on this hallowed ground, we too will be destroyed—just like they were. I don't care if you like each other or not. But you will respect each other. And maybe—I don't know—maybe we'll learn to play this game like men.

Practice Speech: Introduction

Time Limit: 60 seconds

Instructions: Choose a famous person or character and introduce them to your audience. When you introduce someone to an audience, you are typically the conduit. Meaning you have a relationship with the speaker and the audience knows you. Research the person's life and identify the biggest highlights—be sure to include where you found your information. Seek to connect the speaker's highlights, achievements, or insights to the audience's interest or concerns. Not only does this build speaker credibility, but also creates interest for the audience. Begin with an engaging first line and end your speech with a big build such as, "Put your hands together for..." or "Give a warm welcome to.. ." Keep the audience in suspense, even if they know who the guest is; don't reveal the name of the person until you announce their name at the end, build the excitement for a big crescendo. Whomever you select, be sure to conduct some research about them and share with your audience where you obtained the information.

Audience: You serve on a board of your favorite non-profit. This is the big sponsorship gala of the year. The guest speaker is the highlight of the evening and you have the pleasure of ntroducing the individual to the crowd.

Purpose: Make this speech all that it can be. Be creative, incorporate some fun ideas to make the content come alive. Sweeten It—consider every way to make this speech surpass expectations and add Wow Factor".

Skills to Practice: DP4: Sweeten It, DP5: Power of the Pause, DP6: Engage, Engage, Engage.

Sample Speech

Chances are you have welcomed our guest for this evening into your house on many occasions. No doubt, he has delighted your family and friends—he might even have become a regular member of the household as he has mine. Just this morning my five-year-old proclaimed, "What a treat!"

He giggled his **way** into the world in **October** of **1965** created by Rudy Perz (Goodsell, 2011). He is a whopping **14 ounces** and a **lengthy 9** inches. Inventors' expert Mary Belvis (2015) reports that he "originates from Minneapolis, where he lives with his wife, **Mrs. Poppie Fresh**, along with their **two** children Popper **and** Bun Bun."

He is a famous **spokesperson**, icon, mascot, **and** trademark for his **company**. He has been seen in over **600** commercials, advertising more than **50** products. He has been **an** opera singer, rapper, rock star, poet, ballet dancer, and **even** a skydiver (Goodsell, 2011).

His website reports (Goodsell, 2011) that he receives over **200** fan letters **per week**, this superstar has been honored with several awards **including**, "Favorite Spokesperson", "Toy of the Year" **and** "Favorite Food Product Character."

He is **not** considered a very smart **cookie**; he often **wastes** much of his **dough** on **half-baked** schemes. Even though he was a **little flaky** at times, he is still considered a **roll** model for millions.

His most famous quote (Belvis, 2015) is..."**Nothin'** says **lovin'** like **bakin'** in the **oven!**" Ladies and gentleman, please give a "Whoo Hoo" for the Pillsbury Doughboy!

Note: The bold words are selected by the speaker for emphasis.

Note: Notice how citations inserted throughout the speech make the speech more credible.

Everything is important—success is in the details.

– *Steve Jobs*

Chapter 4:
Make Visuals Count

Objectives

By the end of this chapter you should be able to:

1. Compare the value of visuals for presenters vs. the audience.

2. Identify your preferred learning style.

3. List the top mistakes people make creating their slides.

4. Explain why visuals are necessary in presentations.

5. Apply the C^2ARES Concept using a content slide.

6. Call on audience members using WPPR (Word, Point, Probe, Review).

4.1 Presentation Preference

Question: Which of the following presentations would you prefer to attend?

A. Lecture only
B. Lecture supplemented with slides including images and short video or animation
C. Lecture with demonstration
D. Lecture with audience interaction including props
E. All of the above

Types of Slides

Name of Slide	Description
Title	**Names the presentation. (Avoid using during your presentation.)** The default first slide for most slide applications is typically a Title Slide. While it seems to make sense to put a cover on your presentation, if you really think about it, your slides are not a "book" of your presentation, rather they are specific visuals designed to support your presentation. Automatically using a Title Slide can actually harm your presentation. Remember that you need to begin your presentation with a "Wow" factor, a hook or an attention grabber. Can a Title Slide ever really be dynamic and create that great first impression? No, it provides a Title of your presentation and your name. No "WOW" at all. I advise people to follow the Speech Formula and take control of every aspect of how you begin your speech. To do that well, at no point is there any room for a slide that states your name and the name of the speech. There can be situations, where event coordinators may use a Title Slide as a space holder between presenters. In these situations resist the urge to begin your presentation with an underwhelming opener referring to your name and topic. *(Referred to as Title Slide)*
Content	**Presents key information with a descriptive title.** Content slides are crucial for your presentation. They help you stay on point and they help your audience comprehend vital information. Create Content Slides with care. Break down data using key words. Remember the rule of 4 words/4 lines per slide unless a list of information is being presented. Content slides can have one or two areas of content. The two areas allows you to compare and contrast ideas. To make the slide visually appealing remember you can insert images but do so sparingly and always explain what the image is and why it is there. Don't assume your audience has made the same connection that you did. *(Referred to as Title and Content Slide or Comparison Slide or Two Content Slide)*
Transitional	**Transitional slide to indicate a change from one idea to another.** Section Header slides are wonderful to use to transition between Main Points. Displaying the Main Points on one slide and showing that same slide to indicate progression from one point to another helps the audience follow the ideas in your speech. Use the Section Header slide every time you change a point and your audience will know the points of your speech by the end. After all, isn't that the point of the presentation?
Graphic	**Blank slide used to insert an image, graph or media.** Sometimes a picture really can be worth a thousand words. If you find that image, use it! Anytime you have an image explain what it is and why you used it. Don't assume the audience will process it in the same way you have. Graphs displaying data can also be extremely helpful in relaying content. Finally, a short video can be a great way to grasp the audience's attention and help them make sense of information. Warning...I recommend having any videos in a separate browser and just display an image of the video on the slide as a place holder. In my experience about 50% of the time videos embedded in presentations fail to play—even when they have been tested on the equipment. I recommend bypassing the potential problem all together, unless you have experience well beyond mine. *(Referred to as Blank Slide)*

4.2 Explore How Visuals Are Used in Speeches

For each type, answer:

1. Have you seen this type of visual used in a speech or presentation? Yes/No

2. Did the visual work effectively within the speech? Yes/No

3. How often have you seen this type of visuals in a presentation? 1 not very often, 5 commonly used.

4. Have you every used this type of visual in a presentation. Yes/No

Type	Example	Description	Seen Yes	Seen No	Worked Yes	Worked No	Frequency 1 to 5	Used Yes	Used No
1D	One Dimensional								
	Visualization	Getting the audience to close their eyes and envision what you tell them to think.							
	Audio	Frequencies or cymbals in the audible range.							
	Light	Flashing or blinking lights or lights that change color.							

Type	Example	Description	Seen Yes	Seen No	Worked Yes	Worked No	Frequency 1 to 5	Used Yes	Used No
2D	Two Dimensional, having length and width, but no depth.								
	Video	Animations: dynamic visual medium produces from static drawings, modesl or objects that are rapidly sequenced together.							
		Clip (cutting): a portion of the whole							
		Trailer: a short promotional film composed of clips showing highlights of a movie.							
		Talking head: recorded video of a person or persons discussing a topic.							
		News: content portrayed froma news organization.							
		Self-Made Video: recording and editing designated for a defined audience.							
	Internet	a vast computer network linking smaller computer networks worldwide							
		Websites: pages of content portrayed by a specific entity.							
		Internal software designed and written to fulfill a particular purpose the user.							
	Slides	Rectangular surface containing content for the purposes of viewing on a screen. (Static)							
		Too much information (sentences & even paragraphs)							

Type	Example	Description	Seen		Worked		Frequency	Used	
			Yes	No	Yes	No	1 to 5	Yes	No
		Too little information (one word slides)							
		Just the right amount (combination key words brief descriptions (4 words/4 lines)							
	Images	Optical counterpart or appearance of an object. (Static)							
		Printed: produced by applying inked types, plates or the like to paper.							
		Projected: to cause (a figure or image) to appear, as on a background.							
	Charts/ Boards	Allows for viewing and input. (Dynamic)							
		Flipchartflip: a set of sheets, as a cardboard or paper hinged at top so they can be flipped to show information.							
		White/Chalk Board: smooth surface that can be written on with a colored markers or chalk.							

Type	Example	Description	Seen		Worked		Frequency	Used	
			Yes	No	Yes	No	1 to 5	Yes	No
3D	Three Dimensional, having length, width and depth.								
	Model	Representation of a larger item.							
	Objects	Anything that is visible or tangible and is relatively stable in form.							
		Support: Objects used to represent an idea or concept.							
		Real: Demonstration of original object discussed							
	People	Testimonial: Share personal experience							
	People	Role Play: Act out a scripted scene							
		Volunteers: Interact with content							

Type	Example	Description	Seen		Worked		Frequency	Used	
			Yes	No	Yes	No	1 to 5	Yes	No
4D	Four Dimensional								
	Time	3D that changes over time: an action with a 3D object. For example, swinging a bat, throwing a ball.							

Visual   **Auditory**   **Tactile**

4.3 What's Your Learning Style?

You have to make an important speech at a conference or special occasion. You would: (circle which one)

make diagrams or get graphs to help explain things	gather many examples and stories to make the talk real and practical	write out your speech and learn from reading it over several times	write a few key words and practice saying your speech over and over
Visual	Kinesthetic	Read/Write	Aural

Visuals/Slides are a Win-Win

SPEAKER	AUDIENCE
1. They help you, the speaker, break down the content. 2. They serve as a great cue card so you can remember points you want to cover. 3. They provide another dimension to engage the audience.	1. They help the audience comprehend the concepts. 2. The repetition of seeing and hearing help the audience retain the information. 3. They can be entertaining and vary the presentation.

*Note: **Never** have the same content on your cards. This ensures that you interact with the slide, keeping the audience engaged, as opposed to reading content off of cards.*

4.4 Do Slides Help or Hurt?

Think of presentations you have experienced that used visuals. Did the visuals support or detract from the presentation? What are things you have seen presenters do with visuals that help their presentation and vice-versa?

Help	Hurt

Slide Presentation Guidelines

Do	Don't
Engage the audience—individually and as a group for at least $\frac{1}{3}$ of every slide.	Write full sentences and just read off slides.
Cite any ideas that are not your own —both visually and orally.	Turn your back to the audience.
Create powerful audience connection using at least one of the 4Ps for each content slide.	Make a sloppy presentation with unexplained images, overly dark colors, and unclear labels.
Select a light background with dark letters for readability with the lights on.	Turn the lights down for PowerPoint and this lowers the room's energy level.
Include images that match and support theme.	Just flip through the slides and forget about the audience.
Interact with content on the slides. Touch the points or key words for emphasis.	Ignore the visual.
Before you show each slide, grab attention by thoughtful introduction.	Have misspelled words, lack of titles or content on wrong level.
Keep your body facing the audience at *all* times.	Read off the slide word for word.
Explain any images.	Make the same mistakes you have seen other people make with visuals.

Activity

Think about presentation(s) you have observed where a presenter used visuals. List what people did that engaged your attention and what people did to lose your attention.

Description: Create a short (1 minute) presentation incorporating visuals, capturing one chapter objective from a designated chapter from your text (include an APA citation), either a chapter objective from a chapter from your text, or an article about public speaking or a topice relevant to you. Be selective about the content you include. Do not attempt to share too much content. Consider what you have learned: connecting with your audience, your strengths and weaknesses as a speaker, and the delivery principles. Create a presentation you would want to hear! Make it exciting—begin by connecting not stating, "This is Chapter 1". Package the concept and "sell" it to your audience, imagine a commercial. In a presentation, when we have research or content information that can be difficult for an audience to comprehend orally, always visually support your message to help the audience comprehend.

This practice also helps the presenter share the information dynamically, the visual highlights the key points, so you won't have to memorize the content or use cards at all! After your 60-second presentation, ensure that they "got" the information by asking a question about the content.

C^{2}ARES

Check	For each slide	Definition
	CITE	What is your citation? Be sure to include the source site and explain why it's credible.
	CALL	When will you call on the audience? Who will you call upon? Keep your audience involved in the transmission of content during each slide. Remember WPPR: Word, Probe, Phrase, Review.
	ATTENTION GRABBER	How will you intrigue the audience by your transition to this slide content?
	REWARD	How do you intend to reward your audience for their participation? (Besides physical objects, rewards can be verbal acknowledgment or gratitude, but sometime during the presentation, sweeten it to include a physical reward so you can experience how much an audience appreciates that effort.)
	ENGAGE	What will you do to physically involve the audience in your presentation? You can use a prop that reveals content and requires interaction. You can include an activity that requires at least two audience members to move from their seats.
	SLIDE	Break down content so it makes sense. Follow the 4 lines/4 words per line rule, and use light background with dark text.

Remember....C^{2}ARES

Each time you present using a visual be sure to incorporate the C^{2}ARES principle for visual.

Call Rules

Call WPPR (Word, Probe, Point, Review)

WORD	Choose a key word that you want to highlight. Point to the word, and ask everyone together, "What is that word ____?" If their reply is not loud enough, ask them again. Involve a specific audience member to read a point on each slide. (Alternatively, on an important point you can ask the entire audience to state the word(s) aloud—for emphasis repeat…What? (Encourage them to be louder).
PROBE	Ask, "Which of these points do you think is most important?" This works really well with a list. The audience can always read faster than you speak. Let them. This also requires them to engage and think about the content.
POINT	After you share a point, say (or gesture to indicate), "Moving on to the next point…Ashton, can you please read." Then explain or provide an example.
REVIEW (if necessary):	"Skye, what are the 4 techniques to keep your audience awake for your slides?"

Slide Rules: Fundamentals of Creating Slides

DESIGN	1	Choose a background consistent with your message.
	2	Avoid funky colors and fonts.
	3	Make text large enough for easy reading anywhere in the room.
	4	Use a light background and dark letters so slides can be seen with lights up.
CONTENT	5	State your source content in key word format, not full sentences.
	6	Cite sources within the content of your slides for visibility and a reminder to cite orally.
	7	Bulleted lists always have at least two items, preferably three or more.
	8	Keep slide content to four lines or fewer per slide with four words or fewer per line.
DELIVERY	9	Keep the lights up while you present.
	10	Use images consistent with content and explain them.
	11	Use a buddy with whom you have practiced so you can focus on your audience rather then the electronics.
PREPARATION	12	Prepare for Murphy's Law: What can go wrong, will go wrong. Always have a backup plan—test in room if possible. Have slides on USB stick/jump drive, and print presentation in case electronics fail.
	13	Distribute a copy (can be as little as one page) of slides but wait at the end to avoid distracting from your message.

4.5 Finding Mistakes

In this example, see if you can find 3 of the mistakes made.

1.

2.

3.

What is groupthink?

- Groupthink is defective decision making in groups that results from in-group pressure to reach consensus.
- Dr. Janis Arvin refers to Groupthink as " a deterioration of mental efficiency, reality testing, and moral judgment that results from in-group pressure"

- Nietzsche, went so far as to say *"that madness is the exception in individuals but the rule in groups"*

Here are the mistakes we found on the sample slide:

1. Titles are not capitalized. Title should read, "What is Groupthink?"
2. Titles don't represent the content accurately.
   This question listed as the title, "What is groupthink?" is the first main point; whereas the content on the slide relates to the subpoint which is Definintion. Thus the slide title should be "Definition" not "What is groupthink?" Titles should always describe the slide content. If you implement the Speech Formula, your subpoints will consistently be the Titles for your content slides. For instance, in this case the speech shows this skeleton outline:

   I. What is Groupthink?
      A. Definition
      B. Individual vs. Group Decisions
   II. How can we make better decisions as a group?

   Notice how on the corrected version of the slide located in the next section, *How to Improve the Slide*, the sub point is featured to correctly label the slide content, "Definition." The title should consistently feature the sub point as that accurately names the content of the slide.
3. Chunks of information will distract audience and tempt speaker to read slide rather than explaining. Instead, break the information down by creating bullets for key ideas.
4. Citations are inconsistent and wordy. Limit citations on slide to author's last name and the publication date.
5. Lacks images. Visuals such as a cartoon or image of a group listening to a leader would add value to this message.

How to Improve the Slide

   If this presenter had taken more time to analyze the definition of groupthink, and identify what circumstances provoke it, she would better grasp the concept and be able to speak about it extemporaneously without reading the definition. For instance, in this situation Paulus (1994) defines groupthink as "defective decision making in groups that results from in-group pressure to reach consensus." Key words that pop at me in that definition are defective, pressure, and consensus. Having read, analyzed, and written the words I want to use in the speech, when I see this slide featuring these three key words, I can flesh out the thought.

Subpoint

Keywords

Main point

Definition: (Paulus, 1994)

1. Defective decision making
2. Consensus is sought
3. Pressure applied

What is Groupthink?

ALL THOSE IN FAVOUR SAY 'YES'
LeadersLab.co.uk (2015)

4.6 Fix This Slide

Identify at least five things wrong with this slide.

STEPS TO FORGIVENESS	What's Wrong With This Slide:

STEPS TO FORGIVENESS

1) State who and/or what you need to forgive aloud.

   a) This helps in the process of understanding and coming to grips with what the objective is.

2) Acknowledge how you currently feel about the situation. It is best if these are your honest feelings, not the nice, polite things you think you should feel. You need to work from how you really feel. Then you express your willingness to at least be open to the possibility of letting go of those feelings.

3) State the benefits you will get from forgiving. This will mainly be the opposite of what you are currently feeling. Sadness will become happiness, anger will become peace, heaviness becomes a feeling of lightness and so on. If you are not sure about the benefits just choose a few general good feelings which you would like to have for now (happier, more at ease, more confident etc). It helps if you can imagine how much better you will feel when you have forgiven.

4) Commit yourself to forgiving. This is simply stating who you intend to forgive and then acknowledging the benefits which come from forgiving. (martin, william (n.d.). Four Steps to Forgiveness)

What's Wrong With This Slide:

1.

2.

3.

4.

5.

Answers:

1. Way too much information

2. Not chunked, no key words

3. Steps not numbered

4. The source is not credible

5. Not cited correctly in text (author, year)

6. More contrast between background (lighter) and letters (darker)

Create a new slide that follows the rules.

Chapter 4 Review Questions

1. List three reasons why visuals are valuable for both speakers and audience members.

2. List the top mistakes people make creating their slides.

3. List five Do's and Don'ts for making visuals work for you.

4. What is your preferred learning style and how does that reveal itself in your presentations?

5. How can you accommodate multiple learning styles in your speech?

6. Apply the C^2ARES Concept using a content slide.

7. Call on audience members using WPPR.

8. List three disastrous ways to start a speech.

9. Identify five tips you will incorporate when you create your slides.

10. Which quote from this chapter resonates with you the most?

Practice Speech: Interacting with Visuals

Time Limit: Two minutes

Target Audience

Option one: You are asked to present a new procedure to your peers in your office. Legislative compliance requires that the protocol is followed. Be sure your peers can correctly follow the procedure after hearing your presentation. Use a procedure that fulfills a legislative requirement so you can practice citing.

Option two: You are asked to present a research article about public speaking to a group you joined to improve your ability to speak in public. Identify an article and present an overview to the group. Be sure that in your citation you qualify why it is credible information that we should follow.

Instructions:

1. Create a content slide that follows the rules for making your visuals work. You may have a question slide following the content slide.
2. Explain how you intend to implement the C^2ARES Concept using the rubric and reference slide. No more than three total slides: 1. Content Slide, 2. Question Slide, 3. Reference Slide.

Slide #	For each slide	Describe how you will incorporate?
	CITE:	
	CALL:	
	ATTENTION GRABBER:	
	REWARD:	
	ENGAGE:	
	SLIDE:	

3. Practice deliberately making your stretch goal to implement each of the six C^2ARES Concepts
4. Dynamically present the slide, interacting with your audience as expected.
5. Record your presentation and evaluate how well you implemented C^2ARES.

Purpose: To ease into the delivery process by providing a non-threatening venue. Focus on the variety of vocal inflections you use. Project your voice as much as you can. Create excitement by the energy you put into your voice.

Skills to Practice: Employ each part of the C^2ARES concept effectively.

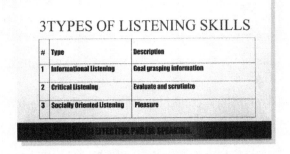

#	Type	Description
1	Informational Listening	Goal grasping information
2	Critical Listening	Evaluate and scrutinize
3	Socially Oriented Listening	Pleasure

3 LISTENING CHALLENGES

1. Message Overload
2. Psychological Noise
3. Lack Of Motivation

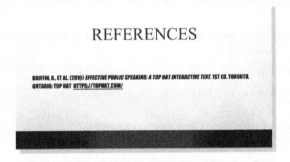

QUESTIONS

What are 3 different types of listening?

List 3 challenges to listening?

(Treats given for correct answers!)

REFERENCES

GRIFFIN, G., ET AL (2016) *EFFECTIVE PUBLIC SPEAKING: A TOP HAT INTERACTIVE TEXT.* 1ST ED. TORONTO, ONTARIO: TOP HAT HTTPS://TOPHAT.COM/

Sample Story: Making Visuals Work for You

Script

This is a sample presentation by Makeda Serju and Fabienne Desir with the help of a buddy in the audience. See how well they incorporated the C2ARES concept.

As Makeda and Fabienne stand before the audience ready to begin, suddenly an audio clip randomly plays from the back of the audience.

Begin with little skit:

Buddy: Start audio clip from the back of the audience.
Both Makeda and Fabienne look at each other confused. Mouthing the words, "What?" Both shrug their shoulders.

Begin Presentation:

Makeda: *Are you really listening to what you are hearing? How good of a listener are you?*

Fabienne: *May I have five volunteers from the audience come to the stage?* Calls on specific individuals.

Instructs volunteers that she will whisper a phrase and each must whisper it into the next person's ear. Fabienne whispered the phrase "blue jeans" in the first volunteer's ear and Makeda announced the message from the last volunteer that travelled down the chain—which was "blue cheese."

Makeda: *See how bad we can be at listening? The first person heard "blue jeans" somehow the message was misheard and the message got messed up.*

Fabienne: Share content for slide #3 being sure to employ C²ARES. See Sample Criteria Listening Skills below.

Makeda: Share content for slide #4 being sure to employ C²ARES. See Sample Criteria Listening Skills below.

Sample Rubric: Listening Skills by Makeda Serju and Fabienne Desir

Slide #	For each slide
1, 2, 3	**CITE:** According to Edward Griffin in the book *Effective Public Speaking*.
2, 3	**CALL:** Slide 3: Call Lily...to read, "Social Oriented Listening." Slide 4: Hand out three posters with the definitions. Poster 1: Someone has so much information that they are unable to deal with it. Poster 2: We come into a conversation with ideas about what the other person is going to say and why, we can easily become blinded to their original message. Poster 3: Absence or deficiency in desire, interest and driving force to hear or follow words.
1	**ATTENTION GRABBER:** Start with the game "Chinese Whispers."
N/A	**REWARD:** Reward the individuals who participated in the game and read the points off the slide with a chocolate turtle. Give everyone a little quote on listening. "When people talk, listen completely. Most people never listen." –Ernest Hemingway "Most people do not listen with the intent to understand; they listen with the intent to reply." –Stephen R. Covey "One of the most sincere forms of respect is actually listening to what another has to say." –Bryant H. McGill "If you make listening and observation your occupation, you will gain much more than you can by talk."–Robert Baden-Powell "Most of the successful people I've known are the ones who do more listening than talking. –Bernard Baruch "The art of conversation lies in listening."–Malcom Forbes "We have two ears and one tongue so that we would listen twice as much as we talk." –Diogenes "You cannot truly listen to anyone and do anything else at the same time." –M. Scott Peck
1	**ENGAGE:** Ask five members of the audience to come to the front. We whispered into the ear of the first one. during the "Chinese Whispers" game. Definition, Poster Slide 4
all	**SLIDE:** Followed the rules, only key words.

> Only when you are aware of the uniqueness of everyone's individual body will you begin to have a sense of your own self-worth.
>
> – Ma Jian

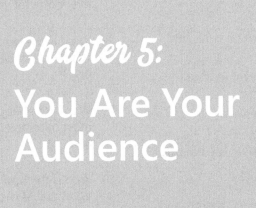

Chapter 5: You Are Your Audience

Objectives

By the end of this chapter you should be able to:

1. Describe why it is important as a speaker to connect with yourself.

2. Explain why taking a personal inventory is vital to your personal awareness.

3. Describe the components of a good personal support system.

4. Identify your most extreme characteristic for each personality test.

5. Share your stories dynamically.

Self Inventory

As you answer these questions on a separate sheet of paper, feel free to think them over, don't try to answer all at one time. Maybe discuss some with people who know you well. Be honest with yourself. It might be beneficial to explore the personality tests as they may reveal some important information about yourself.

1. What are your *five* greatest strengths? What are your *five* biggest weaknesses?

2. When people first meet you, what words would they use to describe you?

3. What words would you use to describe yourself?

4. What *three* things are most important to you?

5. What are your top *three* pet peeves?

6. What is your proudest moment? What is your most embarrassing moment?

7. What are your goals for this day, week, month, and year?

8. How organized are you and how does your organization impact your life?

9. In any given room filled with people, to what extent are you an extravert? What does that mean about how you communicate?

10. How open are you to change compared to other people?

11. What is your learning style preference and to what extent? Think of someone close to you. What is their learning style preference?

12. Do you think more globally (big picture) or sequentially (specifics)?

13. What part of your brain dominates your interactions? How does this compare to other people around you?

14. When is the last time you *really* looked into your own eyes in the mirror? If you haven't, do so. Look closely. Did you like what you saw? What made you uncomfortable or comfortable?

15. What is your personal mission statement? Write one if you don't have one.

16. What is funny to you; what is *not* funny to you?

17. What is the nicest thing you have ever done for someone? What is the *nicest* thing someone has ever done for you?

18. What is the *worst* thing someone has ever done to you? And the *worst* thing you did to somebody else?

19. Who is the happiest person you know? Who is the most miserable? What makes them the way they are?

20. Who is the best communicator you know? What makes them great? Who is the worst communicator? What makes them bad?

21. What are your three best moments in your job?

22. What are five things you do to raise your self-esteem and five things you do to harm your self-esteem?

23. What is your biggest fear?

24. What is your personal favorite quality you possess?

25. What is your favorite picture of yourself?

26. What is the funniest thing you have ever witnessed? When have you laughed the hardest?

27. How often do you laugh? How could you laugh more?

28. Whom in your life do you most admire and why?

29. Who in your life admires you? Why?

30. Describe a time in your life when "you being who you are" opened doors for yourself. When have "you being who you are" *closed* doors for yourself?

5.1 Awareness Traits

Examine the list of signs below. Which of the characteristics below are traits of an aware person and which are traits of unaware people?

	Aware	Unaware
1. Takes Ownership		
2. Open		
3. Trusts Others		
4. Action Meets Word		
5. Makes Excuses		
6. Defensive		
7. Micromanages Situations		
8. Talks More than They Do		

5.2 Social Support

Who are the people who make up the characters in your life?

Beware, you don't have to like or even trust the individuals you list. These are people who "get" your time, for whatever reason. They account for the moments that make up your life. Imagine the tick-tock of the clock... seconds, minutes and hours—to whom do you give those moments? Anyone who captures a portion of your time per week, should be listed. Next list the degree of positive influence they have on your life on a scale of 1-10.

Would they agree? Why would your opinions differ?

PEOPLE IN MY LIFE

NAME	RANK	NAME	RANK

Your Support System

Place the names you listed as your support system in the correct location on this diagram. Be sure to place those that are closest to you on the inner circles and those more distant from you on the outer circles.

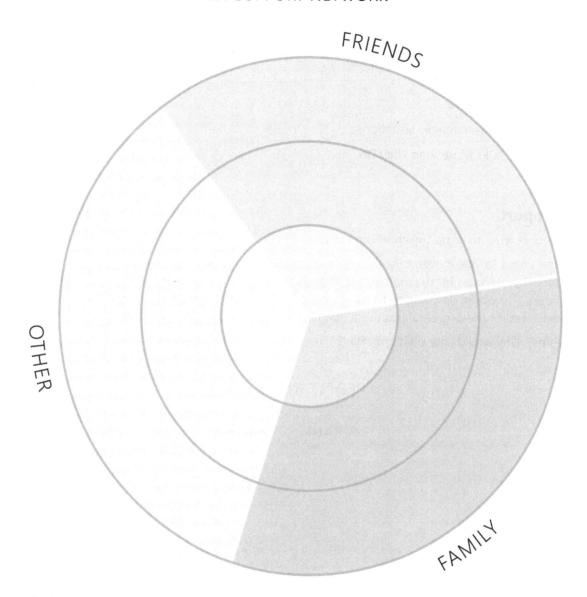

MY SUPPORT NETWORK

FRIENDS

OTHER

FAMILY

Now that you have identified who is in your life and how close these relationships are to you, let's look at the type of support each provides.

Personal Support System Chart

Type	Definition	Example	Who's in my corner?
Emotional	Expressions of comfort and caring	Someone who makes you feel better because they listen to your problems	
Informational	Provision of advice and guidance	A person who can give trusted advice and guidance on an issue	
Tangible	Provision of material aid	A person who could give you a personal financial loan - SOS	
Belonging	Shared social activities, sense of social belonging	A friend with whom you enjoy just hanging out	

Reflection

What have you learned about the people in your life? Are there any adjustments you will make about with whom you share your time? Are the people who provide the most support to you on your inner circle? What type of support are you to the people in your life?

Personality Tests

1. Take each test on line (you can search for them or use the links on Blackboard). Carefully consider what each test measures (READ the descriptions). Print your results (Print screen is fine you can place all on one page.)

2. Circle ANY dimension which you scored 20% or lower on either side of the scale.

3. Digest your results, did you score "extreme" in any dimension? Did you reject any part of the results as being "wrong"? Might someone else identify that quality in you? Try to see how your personality impacts your interactions, for instance if you were to switch results with another how would your life be different?

4. Write a paragraph for EACH test which addresses the following:

   a. Identify a specific time in you r life (not a generic characteristics) when you see one dimension of this test reveal itself in your actions. Use a specific details in this example being sure to include names, dates and places. Note: You will forfeit points if you fail to provide specific example.

   b. How can this insight allow me to better manage my personality?

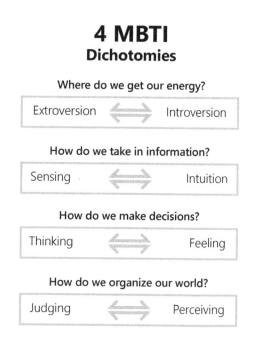

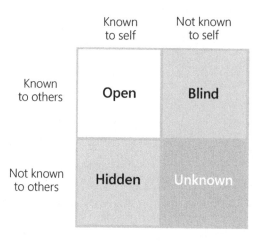

Dr. Carmella's GUIDE TO UNDERSTANDING THE INTROVERTED!

By Roman Jones ©2012

1. WHAT IS INTROVERSION?

INTROVERTED PEOPLE LIVE IN A HUMAN-SIZED HAMSTER BALL. (NOT REALLY, BUT YOU KNOW WHAT I MEAN)
THE MAJOR TRAIT OF A TRUE INTROVERT, AS OPPOSED TO SOMEONE WHO IS WITHDRAWN, IS HOW THEY GAIN THEIR ENERGY.

EXTROVERTED PEOPLE GATHER THEIR ENERGY FROM THEIR SURROUNDINGS.
THEY ABSORB THE "GOOD VIBES" OF THE PEOPLE AROUND THEM AND THUS NEED A LOT OF SOCIAL INTERACTION.

I'D BETTER GET HOME AND READ SOME BOOKS

INTROVERTED PEOPLE MAKE THEIR OWN ENERGY AND, RATHER THAN TAKING IT FROM OTHERS, GIVE IT ON SOCIAL CONTACT.

THIS MEANS THAT THEY NATURALLY FIND MOST INTERACTION EXHAUSTING AND NEED TIME TO RECHARGE.

ENERGY BUCKET

BECAUSE THIS ENERGY IS A LIMITED RESOURCE, THEY TEND TO SEE EXTROVERTS AS OBNOXIOUS PREDATORS OUT TO STEAL THEIR SWEET, SWEET ENERGY JUICES.
THAT'S WHY THEY HAVE THE HAMSTER BALL OF PERSONAL SPACE.

COME OUT!

HISSS...

2. HOW TO INTERACT WITH THE INTROVERTED

JUST BECAUSE SOMEONE IS INTROVERTED DOESN'T MEAN THEY DON'T LIKE COMPANY.
INTERACTION IS JUST EXPENSIVE AND THEY DON'T WANT TO SPEND IT ON SOMETHING ANNOYING (READ: WASTEFUL)
HERE'S WHAT YOU DO:

HELLO

HI

SAY HELLO, BE POLITE AND RELAXED, SHOW THAT YOU RECOGNIZE AND APPROVE OF THEIR PRESENCE.
IT IS IMPORTANT FOR INTROVERTS TO FEEL WELCOME - THEY WON'T SPEND THEIR PRECIOUS ENERGY ON SOMEONE WHO DOESN'T WANT THEM AROUND.
IF YOU HAVE INTERESTING/IMPORTANT NEWS TO MENTION, MENTION IT. JUST DON'T PRESS FOR GOSSIP.

THEN GO BACK TO WHATEVER YOU WERE DOING.
NOW THE INTROVERTS KNOW THAT YOU ARE FRIENDLY AND OPEN TO INTERACTION BUT WILL NOT PUSH THEM INTO SPENDING ENERGY IF THEY HAVE NO NEED TO.

TAH-DAH! THAT'S ALL THERE IS TO IT!

REMEMBER:

- RESPECT PERSONAL SPACE (HAMSTER BALL)
- ENERGY IS LIMITED
- DON'T DEMAND TO HAVE ENERGY SPENT ON YOU WHEN IT'S NOT PARTICULARLY NEEDED
- DON'T TAKE SILENCE AS AN INSULT - IT ISN'T!
- INTROVERTS GET LONELY, TOO

THAT'S IT, FOLKS!
BE SURE TO HUG YOUR INTROVERTS TODAY!
(WITH PERMISSION, OF COURSE.)

5.3 Personality and Job Performance

Mark true or false:

_____ Knowing your personality type gives you a huge advantage in the workplace.

_____ Most high performers know their personality type.

_____ Ninety percent of Fortune 500 companies and MBA programs use personality type testing to help people reach their potential.

5.4 Empower Your Inner Narrative

Identify a story in your life that could use a facelift. Follow Hyatt's five steps to create a more empowering narrative. (Refer to the Practice Speech: My Favorite Story for specific instructions and additional resources to complete this activity.)

Businessman and author, Michael Hyatt (2017) in his article "What Story Are You Telling Yourself?" encourages readers to create more empowering inner narratives by following five steps:

1. **Become aware of the Narrator.** Half the battle is simply waking up and becoming conscious of the commentary running through our minds. Most people are oblivious to it. It is especially important to be alert to it whenever we experience adversity or trauma. Ask: Am I telling myself a story right now?

2. **Write down what the Narrator says.** When the story starts playing, take a minute and jot it down. Try to get it word-for-word. It could be, "I'm not a gifted public speaker." Or, "I'll never reach my goals." Or, "He'll never go out with a person like me." Whatever the story is, get it down. Ask: What is the story am I telling myself right now?

3. **Evaluate the story the Narrator is telling.** It's easy to confuse the Narrator's voice with the Truth. But the Narrator is only offering one perspective, based on previous experiences and—too often—fear. We don't have to accept the version of reality the Narrator is telling, especially if it's disempowering and prevents us from reaching our goals. Ask: Is this storyline just a limiting belief?

4. **Affirm what you know is true.** You can either live life based on past experiences, current feelings, or the Truth. As one of my mentors often says, "Most people doubt their beliefs and believe their doubts. Do just the opposite." Ask: What do I know to be true?

5. **Write a new script.** We don't have to be passive spectators in our stories; we certainly don't have to be victims. Our choices matter—more than we think! They can affect the outcome. Ask: How can I make the choices that create the best possible story?

Chapter 5 Review Questions

1. Why it is important as a speaker to connect with yourself?

2. What question in your inventory was the most interesting for you to answer? Which question was the most difficult to answer?

3. What can you do to enhance your social support system?

4. Which of the personality tests is the most known?

5. What is the difference between an introvert and an extrovert?

6. Which is more important: Identifying which trait you are or identifying where you fall on the scale?

7. Identify your most extreme characteristic for each personality test.

8. Which test held the most significance for you? Why?

9. Identify at least two ways that stories can serve as powerful tools.

10. Which quote from this chapter resonates with you the most?

Practice Speech: My Favorite Story

Time Limit: 90 seconds

Audience: You are at dinner with a group of friends and/or family. Someone references an event and you have the perfect story to augment the conversation.

Instructions:

1. Choose a story you love! What's your favorite story? Why do you like it?

2. Consider your audience.

3. Identify the reason for sharing. What is the moral of the story?

4. Write the story. Include vivid details: who, what, where, when, how and why. Find the right amount, not too much, not too little. Be sure you include a hook, emphasize the conflict, and conclude with impact. Be vulnerable open up about your experience.

5. Practice speaking the story. Tell it often.

Purpose: Examine your stories; rewrite the script if necessary. Practice your ability to speak about yourself personally. Practice the art of telling a story.

Skills to practice: DP2: Project, DP5: Pause, DP6: Engage, DP9: Dance.

Resources:

- How to Tell a Great Story: https://theartofcharm.com/self-mastery/how-to-tell-a-great-story/?hvid=3q1eB7
- WikiHow: Tell a Story: http://www.wikihow.com/Tell-a-Story
- Harvard Business Review: How to Tell a Great Story https://hbr.org/2014/07/how-to-tell-a-great-story

Example: Sorry, this is your story! It just doesn't work if you tell somebody else's.

Practice Speech: Who Am I?

Time Limit: Three minutes

Audience: You have decided to take the trip of a lifetime, sailing as a passenger through the Greek Islands for a month without anyone you know. Nine other people that have chosen the same vacation. You come together for a meet-and-greet. Directly afterward, you attend an orientation where each passenger must deliver a short speech by briefly explaining who they are and sharing a significant story that was instrumental in molding their character.

Instructions:

1. Think of your life on a timeline.
2. Consider your audience.
3. Identify the key moments you will highlight.
4. Create some tension by revealing a struggle you had and how you resolved it.
5. Construct the story being sure to share vivid details: who, what, where, how and why. Be vulnerable open up about your experience. Include a hook, emphasize the conflict, and conclude with impact. Consider if it is the right length.
6. Practice telling the story as often as possible.

Purpose: Examine your stories; rewrite the script if necessary. Practice your ability to speak about yourself personally. Practice the art of telling a story.

Skills to Practice: DP2: Project, DP5: Pause, DP6: Engage, DP9: Dance.

Example: Sorry, this is your story! It just doesn't work if you tell somebody else's.

Practice Speech: Pitch/Elevator

Time Limit: 60 seconds

Audience: You are walking down the hallway at work and see the elevator doors begin to close. You hurry and just manage to stop the doors from closing. As they reopen, you're stunned to see the owner of the company you have been dreaming of working for standing on the elevator. Thank goodness, you are on the 36th floor. You have sixty seconds to inspire the owner to read your resume and request an interview.

Instructions:

1. Determine your purpose. What do you want to have happen by the end of the pitch? An interview? Submitting a business card? A sale?

2. Write the elevator speech.

   a. Set the Stage. Smile – Attention Grabber. Killer first line.

   b. Who are you? What do you do? Be enthusiastic!

   c. What makes you unique? What's next? Share contributions you have made or problems you've solved. Provide an example. Consider audience. What makes you the best?

   d. Engage with a question. Call for action!

3. Establish a deliberate practice to nail this pitch!

4. Tailor your pitch to different audiences.

Purpose: To fine tune your personal branding pitch.

Skills to Practice: DP1: Set the Stage. DP2: Project DP3: Assess and Cope DP6: Engage, Engage, Engage

Resources:

- How to Write a Killer Elevator Pitch - https://theinterviewguys.com/write-elevator-pitch/

- Your Elevator Pitch Needs an Elevator Pitch - https://hbr.org/2014/12/your-elevator-pitch-needs-an-elevator-pitch

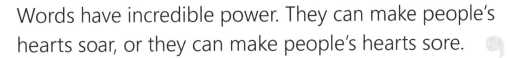

"Words have incredible power. They can make people's hearts soar, or they can make people's hearts sore.
— *Dr. Mardy Grothe*"

Chapter 6:
Your Audience Writes the Speech

Objectives

By the end of this chapter you should be able to:

1. Draw Maslow's hierarchy of needs.

2. Distinguish between the primary audience analysis, the secondary audience analysis and formal audience analysis.

3. Consider how you can respectfully communicate with people who have differing values, beliefs and attitudes.

4. Describe the components of a good personal support system.

5. Explain what it means to be an audience centered communicator.

6. Describe the significance of establishing a meaningful connection (lock) between the audience, yourself and the content.

Define the following words:

Values	
Beliefs	
Attitudes	
Actions	

Draw a tree.
Label: roots, trunk, branches and fruit.
Match: values, beliefs, attitudes and actions.

6.1 Audience Application

Review section 6 Part 1 about Maslow's Hierarchy of Needs and identify three instances where the audience dictated what was written.

1.

2.

3.

BEING NEEDS

Self-actualization

Esteem Needs

Belonging needs

Safety needs

Physiological needs

DEFICIT NEEDS

Practice Speech: Same Speech, Two Audiences

Time Limit: 3-5 minutes

Topic: Choose a topic, issue, or experience in which you have some expertise. If you have none, choose the drinking age.

Audience #1: The Kiwanis club closest to your house needs a speaker for their weekly meeting. They are trying to gain insight into people in their community.

Audience #2: The local YMCA has a community fair that young adults will attend to gather tips about life. You have been invited to present a session.

Instructions: Conduct a Primary Audience Analysis and Secondary Audience Analysis for both of these audiences.

Purpose: Examine how your Primary Audience Analysis questions illuminate why audiences need to be approached differently even with the same topic.

Example: Provided in the chapter between the Executive Group of Women and Juvenile Girls.

Topic _____

Primary: Kiwanis	Primary: YMCA
1.	1.
2.	2.
3.	3.
4.	4.
Secondary: Kiwanis	Secondary: YMCA
1. Why is the topic important?	1. Why is the topic important?
2. How will they benefit?	2. How will they benefit?
3. What will they learn?	3. What will they learn?

> It takes one hour of preparation for each minute of presentation time.
>
> – *Wayne Burgraff*

Chapter 7:
Speech Formula

Objectives

By the end of this chapter you should be able to:

1. Distinguish between the primary, secondary and formal audience analysis.

2. List the five rules for creating a statement that has a clear purpose.

2. Explore how the outline works to optimize your speech.

4. Discover how each part of the introduction secures the audience attention.

5. Discuss how the introduction and the conclusion differ.

7.1 Speech Ingredients

What are the ingredients for a good speech? Examine speeches you have heard and speeches you have presented, construct a list of ingredients you think belong in a speech. Be sure to look at the Sample Listening Speech on page 69 to experience the Speech Formula.

Note: Brainstorming with a buddy is great way to answer this question well.

Informative Speech Topic Ideas

Topic	Expert
Birth Order Theory	Alfred Adler
Culture	Edward T. Hall, *Context* Geert Hofstede, *Cultural Dimensions*
Finding Your Voice	Elisabeth Noelle-Neumann, *Finding Your Voice* Irving Janis, *Spiral of Silence & Group Think*
Grit	Angela Duckworth, *The Power of Passion and Perseverance*
Habits	Stephen R. Covey, *7 Habits of Highly Successful People*
Happiness	Marci Shimoff, *Happy for No Reason*
Lying	Pamela Myers, *How to Spot a Liar*
Love	John Lee, *Styles of Love* Robert Sternberg, *Triangular Theory* Gary Chapman, *5 Languages of Love*
Marriage	John Gottman, *4 Horsemen of the Apocalypse*

Speech Formula

Audience Analysis	Purpose Statement	Introduction	Body	Conclusion (Intro backwards)
Primary: Who is my audience? Not about topic!	**1. Use words,** "By the end of my speech my audience will..."	**Attention Grabber** Special, interesting & provocative have them at "Hello!"	Which organizational strategy works BEST to support my purpose? **Select Organizational Strategy**	**Review Main Points** Last opportunity to ensure audience got your points!
Ask questions re: demographics, psychographics or behaviors.	**2. Dream!** GO BIG! What would you like to occur?	**Thesis**	**Create a Skeleton Outline:** I. II. A. A. B. B.	**Restate Thesis**
Secondary: WIFM, connects speaker, message and audience.	**3. KISS:** Keep it simple, 1 idea, no 'and's or conjunctions.	**1. Relate:** Ask probing questions	**Fill out Skeleton Outline** For each sub point break out: 1. Source 2. Connection	**3. Return to Thesis Statement**
1. Why is this topic important to them?	**4. Use active verbs**— something you can physically do!	**2. State:** State your thesis.Modify your purpose statement.	**1. Source:** Write what you will say to your audience about your sub point. Include quality research and be credible, cite.	**2. Return to Thesis Statement**
2. How will my audience benefit from my words?	**5. Do not share in this form with audience.** You will repurpose for your thesis statement	**3. Quote:** Use a quote written by someone famous to support value of speech.	**2. Connection:** For each sub point, make the information come alive by making it fun and interesting using the 4Ps Personal Story, Probe, Physical Activity, Prop 3D)	**1. Relate: Ask probing questions.**
3. Will they learn something new?		**Preview Main Points** One sentence, literally copy/paste your Main Points!	**Transitions:** Create transitions to guide the audience from one point to another.	**Return to Attention Grabber** It's an art; bring them full circle!
Formal: Conduct a pre-speech questionnaire.			Write out source, connections and transitions for each sub point.	**Call to Action** (Persuasive speech only)

Speech Process

Phase 1: Planning	Phase 2: Preparation	Phase 3: Construction	Phase 4: Delivery	Phase 5: Reflection
		F4: Body (Write)	**Before Speech**	**After Speech**
• Request	Conduct research	Source: Write source content - cite	• Read speech out loud 5-10	• Secure audience feedback
• Assessment	**F1: Audience Analysis**	Connections: Incorporate the 4 Ps	• Create your cards & visuals	• Reflect upon your delivery
• Schedule	**F2: Purpose Statement**	Transitions: Guide between points	• Practice deliberately with Plan of Action	• Watch video
• Topic	**F4: Body (Organize)**	**F3: Introduction**	• Practice reducing anxiety	• Create an Improvement Plan
	• Select emotional and motivational appeal	**F5: Conclusion**	• Time your speech	• Any opportunities to deliver speech again?
	• Select *best* Organizational Strategy	• Check Formula	• A/V analysis	
	• Skeleton outline	• Sweeten It!	• Prepare evaluations	
		• Solicit feedback	• 25 hour check—*Ready*	
			During Speech	
			• Reduce anxiety	
			• Arrive early	
			• Test A/V equipment	
			• Assess yourself	
			• Record speech	
			• Set the Stage – Do IT!	

Note: F=Formula. F1: Audience Analysis; F2: Purpose Statement; F3: Introduction; F4: Body; F5: Conclusion

Sample Speech: Listening Can Change Your Life

Audience Analysis

Primary Audience Analysis

1. What is the youngest member of my audience vs. the oldest?
2. Are there more males or females?
3. How many is English their second language? How many co-cultures?
4. How many other religions than Christian are represented?
5. What income levels are represented in my audience? Who is the wealthiest, who is the poorest?
6. Who in my audience is most like me? Most unlike me? Why? How?
7. Is anyone in my audience living an alternative lifestyle? How?

Secondary Audience Analysis

1. Why is this topic important to them?
   Listening is the most essential part of communicating.

2. How will my audience benefit from my words?
   *They can engage in every conversation they have better, making the person they speak with feel **great** and learn to learn more from others. Become better observers of the world. Get over themselves **more**.*

3. What new information will they learn?
   *A tangible skill set to listen **better**.*

Formal Audience Analysis

1. How important is listening to the communication process?
2. Are you a better listener or speaker?
3. How often do you believe people fail to listen to others?
4. How would people you listen to, rate you as a listener?
5. How would you rate yourself as a listener 1-10?

Purpose Statement: By the end of my speech the audience will listen more competently.

Introduction

Attention Grabber: Movie clip from "Hitch" http://www.youtube.com/watch?v=-n6ehVRzA-s

Thesis

Relate (Probe): Think with me for a second...who is the best listener you know? Picture this person clearly in your mind. Okay, now think of the worst listener you know. Now, how do you think **you** rate as a listener?

State: Today I would like to talk to you about how to listen more competently.

Support: Many people have spoken wise words about listening. My favorite is a quote from Brenda Ueland, printed in a 1938 Ladies Home Journal issue: "Listening is a magnetic and strange thing, a creative force. The friends who listen to us are the ones we move toward. This is the reason: When we are listened to, it creates us, makes us unfold and expand."

Preview Main Points: Let's explore two questions, #1: What is listening? and #2: How can we improve our listening skills? (Display these two main points on a PowerPoint slide to accommodate different learning styles and emphasize key points.)

Skeleton Outline:

I. What is listening?
   a. Definition
   b. Myths
   c. Facts

II. How can we improve our listening skills?
   a. Awareness
   b. Tips

Body

I. What is listening? To understand what listening is, we need to explore the meaning of three key vocabulary words associated with listening: hearing, listening and active listening.

   A. Definitions:
      1. Source: Pearson, Nelson, Titsworth and Harter (2008) in the popular communication text book, Human Communication, define hearing as "the act of ear receiving sound." So, someone who is deaf cannot receive sound. They (Pearson, et al, 2008) go on to define listening as "the active process of receiving, constructing meaning from, and responding to spoken and/or nonverbal messages." Perhaps this why Harvey Robbins (1992) reports that listening is often a skill that is acquired. "Isn't it ironic, that the areas that we spend the most time, speaking and listening are the areas in which we are least trained? Listening is the most challenging of the communication skills and the most frequently ignored." (Display an abbreviated version with key words on a slide to support different types of learners—include all three words.)

Key Word	Definition	Description
Hearing	Act of receiving sound. (Pearson, et. al, 2008)	A deaf person ear drums cannot receive sound. Nephew Kyle = Amazing Deaf American Ninja Warrior!
Listening	Active process of • receiving, • constructing meaning from, • responding to spoken and/or nonverbal messages"(Pearson, et. al, 2008)	Skill that is acquired (Robbins, 1985).

      2. Connection:

         (Probe) How many of you have been in a situation where you heard a friend speak? When they finished speaking, they asked you a question or sought your advice, and you couldn't respond because you realized you had not listened carefully.

         (Personal) Personally, after I choose this topic I was trying to analyze my own listening skills. I clearly recall a recent conversation with my friend Zhenya. She was trying to explain a serious money problem that could cause her to have to move back to Russia. As she spoke, my mind wandered to other things. When she asked me for advice, I could not respond, because I had not listened to her. I was thinking about something else. I felt so embarrassed. I really did not mean to hurt her, but it looked like I didn't care.

Transition: Current research attempts to resolve this situation by highlighting the process of active listening.

   Cornell University professor Judi Brownell (1985), the author of two books on listening, distinguishes active listening as "an intent to listen for meaning." It is a structured way of listening and responding to others." In this transaction, listeners' attention is focused on the speaker. For this focus to occur, listeners must suspending their own frame of reference and refrain from judgment to fully understand the speaker. As a result, Brownell points out, speakers will be free to fully express themselves without becoming defensive. The good news is that most anyone can learn to become an active listener with practice.

Key Word	Definition		Description
Active Listening	• intent to find meaning • structured	• focus on speaker • no judgment (Brownell, 1985)	Skill Anyone can learn!

Transition: Now that we understand these key words, I would like to share some common myths about listening.

   B. **Myths:** Take a moment to review this list—are there any items on here that you believe to be true about listening?

70

1. Source

Common Listening Myths Steil, L. K., Summerfield, J., & De, M. G. (1985)	
Myth #1: Listening is largely a matter of intelligence.	*Myth #5:* *Learning to read is more important than learning to listen.*
Myth #2: Listening ability is closely related to hearing acuity.	*Myth #6:* *People can will themselves to listen well when they want.*
Myth #3: Daily listening eliminates the need for training.	*Myth #7: Listening is a passive activity and the responsibility is on the sender.*
Myth #4: Our educational system taught us how to listen well.	

2. **Connection:** So which myth stood out to you? Michael? #1. I agree, many smart people have way too much to say! Anyone else? For me Myth #4 stood out. It made me wonder why our schools don't teach and require listening competency. What's the last course on listening you attended?

Transition: I will provide a copy of these myths for your review in my handout at the end of the presentation. For now, let's conclude this section by considering a few facts about listening.

C. Facts

1. **Source:** *Get In Front Communications (Piombino, 2013),* highlights some current facts about current communication. Let's see if you can determine fact from fiction! Have one slide that says Fact or Fiction. Place each of these bullets on individual slides (given that it is a game, cite on the last slide where you reveal the answers.)

   • We listen to people at a rate of 125-250 words per minute, but think at 1,000-3,000 words per minute.

   • Less than two percent of people have had any formal education on how to listen.

   • Images go into your long-term memory, whereas words live in your short-term memory.

   • 55 percent of a message's meaning comes from the speaker's facial expressions, 38 percent from tone and inflection, and seven percent from the actual words spoken.

   • The ability to communicate (listening is a vital part) is crucial for promotion, more important than drive or numbers (Harvard Business Review).

2. **Connection:** (Physical) With slide displayed, ask audience to stand if they believe the statement to be a fact and to remain sitting if they believe it to be fiction. Alternative suggestion: Ask for three volunteers to join you on stage. Instruct the volunteers to move their body to right side of the room if they believe the statement to be a Fact and to the left if they believe it to be Fiction Have the audience call out the statement. All are facts (if you want to put a false fact in—you can always do so). At the end share the whole list and explain that all are facts and provide the citation. Ask volunteers to sit.

   Look at list. (Probe) How can these facts affect your ability to listen? (Wait for a response—share my opinion… #1 helps to explain why it is difficult to truly focus on what another person is saying, our brain works faster than their mouth!

Transition: Given this information we have covered thus far, do you feel that you have a better understanding of what listening is? Great! Let's move on to our second question. Show Main points on PP.

II. **How can we improve our listening skills?**

A. **Awareness, question your ability to listen.**

1. **Source:** Judi Brownell (2015) states that the first step to improving our listening skills begins by questioning our own ability to listen. Listening is so important it is the basis of human interaction. As Susie Mitchell Cortright (2001) points out: "Listening makes our loved ones feel worthy, appreciated, interesting, and respected. Ordinary conversations emerge on a deeper level, as do our relationships. When we listen, we foster the skill in others by acting as a model for positive and effective communication."

2. **Connection:** (Personal) Believe it or not, I equate listening with respect. I have been in situations where I heard what the person is saying, but really was sending messages to wrap it up, so I could make my point. I realize, I can listen better. Awareness involves developing a personal awareness in regards to your own ability to listen. You must be willing to find opportunities to improve. Furthermore, you must have a desire to really hear what others say. We can always improve. Just think, do you feel respected when you're ignored, or someone pretends like they are listening, or seems anxious for you to shut up so they can begin making their own point? I don't. But, in the moment, it is easy to anticipate another's words to get to your point faster. I yearn to slow down and respectfully listen to others even more. How?

Transition: I was happy to discover some strategies in my research to improve my listening skills. The second thing we can do to improve our listening skills is to...

B. **Practice active listening skills.**

1. **Source:** Susie Mitchell Cortright (2001) describes 10 tips to practice active listening skills. Review this list! Which of these will be easy to master? Which will be difficult?

Tip	Description
1. Face the speaker	Sit up straight or lean forward slightly, using body language to show your attentiveness.
2. Maintain eye contact	To a comfortable degree.
3. Minimize external distractions	Turn off the TV. Put down your book or magazine, and ask the speaker and other listeners to do the same.
4. Respond appropriately	Raise your eyebrows. Say words such as "Really," "Interesting," as well as more direct prompts: "What did you do then?" and "What did she say?"
5. Focus solely on what the speaker is saying.	Try not to think about what you are going to say next. The conversation will follow a logical flow after the speaker makes her point.
6. Minimize internal distractions.	If your own thoughts keep horning in, simply let them go and continuously re-focus your attention on the speaker, much as you would during meditation.
7. Keep an open mind.	Wait until the speaker is finished before deciding whether you agree or disagree. Try not to make assumptions about what the speaker is thinking.
8. Avoid letting the speaker know how you handled a similar situation.	Unless they specifically ask for advice, assume they just need to talk it out.
9. Even if the speaker is launching a complaint against you, wait until they finish to defend yourself.	The speaker will feel as though their point has been made. They won't feel the need to repeat it, and you'll know the whole argument before you respond. Research shows that, on average, we can hear four times faster than we can talk, so we have the ability to sort ideas as they come in... and be ready for more.
10. Engage yourself.	Ask questions for clarification, but, once again, wait until the speaker has finished. That way, you won't interrupt their train of thought. After you ask questions, paraphrase their point to make sure you understood. Start with: "So you're saying...?"

2. **Connection:** Each day I have been practicing one strategy and have been amazed at the how my relationships have changed! It is as if there is another dimension added to my interactions. Just Tuesday, I was talking with Coach Steele about my speech—truthfully, I was really proud of it because I worked hard. Rather than the praise I expected, she offered critique on a section. When this happens in my life, my normal instinct is to deny or explain what I meant. Instead, I swallowed my words, consciously opened my ears, and practiced Mitchell's active listening skill #9. Guess what? After a moment, my ears did open, and I heard what

she was saying. As a result, I eliminated two minutes from the speech. Now it makes more sense, and I am happier with it. Initially, I really wanted to defend my reasoning. If I had, I would have missed a valuable lesson. I wonder how many valuable lessons I've missed by trying to defend myself?

Conclusion

Review Main Points: What were the two points we covered today? (Reward audience/Show on PP)
What is listening? How you can become a better listener?

Review Thesis (Return to **each**)

Support: Remember how Brenda Euland points out that, "Listening is a magnetic and strange thing, a creative force. The friends who listen to us are the ones we move toward. When we are listened to, it creates us, makes us unfold and expand."

State: Thus by incorporating these skills in our lives, we can be the creative force that helps those around us expand by listening more competently.

Relate: And, in so doing you can avoid being someone who is a bad listener and perhaps...you can even be someone who listens like this.

Return to Attention Grabber: Replay Hitch video.

7.2 Audience Analysis

Complete your Primary, Secondary and Formal Audience Analysis.

Primary: Write six questions to explore who your audience is, use demographics, psychographics, geography and behaviors, to form questions.

1.

2.

3.

4.

5.

6

Secondary: Answer the following questions:

1. Why is the topic important to my audience?

2. How will they benefit?

3. What new information will they learn?

Formal:
Write 3-5 questions about your topic to explore your audience's views and experiences.

List of Active Verbs

Discover the best word to use for your Purpose Statement.

Abandon	Decide	Guide	Prepare
Abolish	Deduct	Handle	Present
Accelerate	Delegate	Help	Preside
Achieve	Delineate	Identify	Process
Acquire	Deliver	Illustrate	Produce
Act	Describe	Imitate	Program
Adapt	Design	Implement	Promote
Add	Detect	Improve	Provide
Adjust	Determine	Increase	Pursue
Administer	Develop	Induce	Question
Advance	Devise	Influence	Realize
Analyze	Diagnose	Inform	Recommend
Answer	Dictate	Inspire	Reconcile
Approach	Direct	Instigate	Record
Arrange	Discard	Interpret	Redeem
Ascertain	Discover	Investigate	Reduce
Assemble	Display	Lead	Regain
Assess	Dramatize	Maintain	Relate
Attain	Edit	Manipulate	Relax
Avert	Engage	Measure	Report
Budget	Enter	Mediate	Represent
Build	Equip	Mentor	Research
Calculate	Establish	Mobilize	Respond
Catch	Estimate	Monitor	Respond
Classify	Evaluate	Motivate	Reveal
Coach	Examine	Negotiate	Review
Command	Expand	Observe	Schedule
Communicate	Expedite	Obtain	Select
Compile	Experiment	Offer	Submit
Compose	Explain	Operate	Summarize
Conduct	Flout	Order	Supervise
Conserve	Formulate	Organize	Supply
Consolidate	Furnish	Oversee	Support
Construct	Gain	Perceive	Synthesize
Control	Gather	Perform	Systematize
Coordinate	Generate	Persuade	Teach
Counsel	Give	Pick	Treat
Create	Grasp	Pile	Unite
Deal	Grow	Predict	Vanquish

Follow these five rules to develop your Purpose Statement:

1. Begin with the phrase, "By the end of my speech my audience will ..." This focuses your attention on the outcome. It's crucial to begin by focusing on what's most important.

2. Dream big! Imagine that you could grant a wish to each audience member regarding your topic. What result would you like to create? How would the information you share improve their life? What would you offer each audience member if you could? Convey this in your dream. To hear this message anyone should want to listen to your speech; it should be inspirational.

3. Keep It Simple Stupid (KISS!). Limit this statement to one idea, not multiple points. It should not contain conjunctions (and, but, for, or, yet). Think of it as the title above a list of your main points. This single sentence should describe the outcome rather than specific points you will cover. Eliminate the excess words, "be able to" just go to the dream.

4. Use an active verb—something you can physically do! You may only select one verb. Avoid these words: know, understand, or learn. For a list of active verbs refer to Table 7.4.

5. This purpose statement is a tool for you, not intended to be shared with the audience. You will convert this content into for your thesis statement by changing the beginning phrase.

7.3 Purpose Statement

Write a purpose statement for your topic. See list of Active Verbs on the following page.

By the end of my speech my audience will:

7.4 Choose the Best Strategy for This Purpose

Suppose you had a speech whose purpose was: By the end of the speech my audience will donate twenty dollars to help find a cure for cancer. Choose three strategies you could use—which would work best?
Suppose you had a speech whose purpose was: By the end of my speech my audience will appreciate classical music. Choose three strategies you could use—which would work best?

1.

2.

3.

Organizational
Strategies

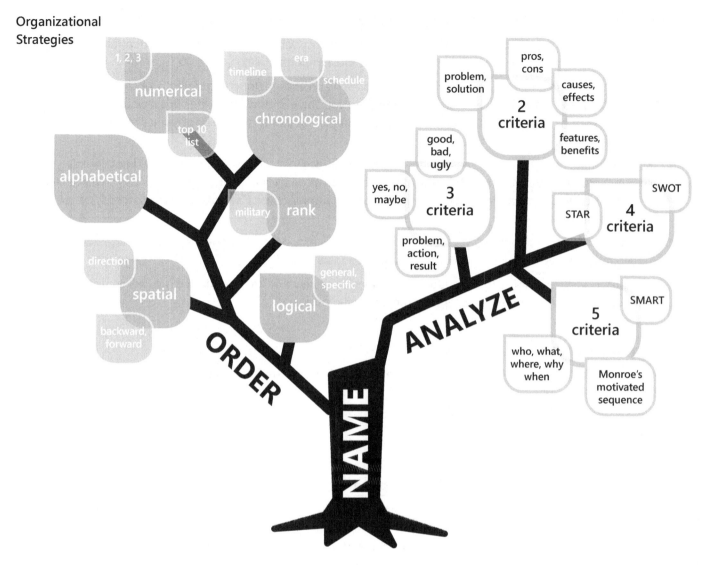

7.5 Body Skeleton Outline

Construct a skeleton outline for a speech for your speech topic.*

Write your Skeleton Outline (Outline your Main Points and Sub Points— use Roman Numerals add any additional points you need as necessary.)

Recommendation: To simplify the process of using the Speech Formula to write this first speech, use these main points as your organizational strategy: I. What is ____? and II. How is it used?

I. What is love?

II. How can we find the love we want?

If your selected topic has more than a word, like, "why marriages fail" as opposed to "happiness", modify it. For instance notice how the second option is a much better outline:

I. What is a marriage?

II. How do we stay married?

I. Why do marriages fail?

II. How can we build lasting relationships?

Construct a skeleton outline for a speech for your speech topic.*

I.
    A.
    B.

II.
    A.
    B.

Appeal Types

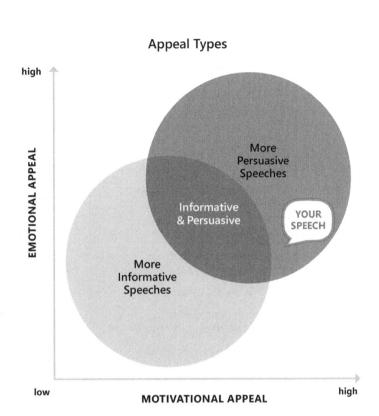

Speech Type by Appeal

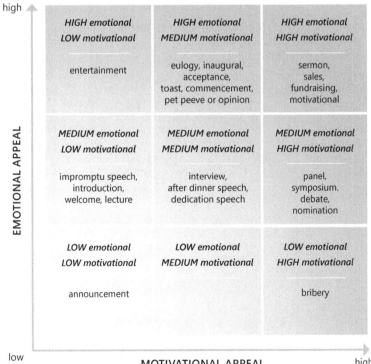

Select Organizational Strategies

INFORMATIVE

Order Strategies

- Letter (A, B, C)
- Timeline (1800, 1900, 2000)
- Era (Big Band, Rock, Hip Hop)
- Schedule (morning, afternoon, evening)
- Military (General, Captain, Lieutenant)
- Corporate (President, Vice President, Manager)
- Government (President, Vice President, Secretary)
- Direction (north, south, east, west)
- Orientation (top, middle, bottom; head, shoulders, knees, toes)
- Internal, External (inside, outside)
- Vertical (Y), Horizontal (X)
- Backward, Forward
- Ingredients, Utensils, Directions
- Color (blue, red)
- Size (small, medium, large) general, specific macro (big picture), micro (small picture)

Analyze Strategies

- Causes, Effects
- Works, Doesn't Work
- Who, What, Where, Why, When

INFORMATIVE AND PERSUASIVE

Order Strategies

- Sequential (1, 2, 3)
- Motivated Sequence (step 1, step 2, step 3)
- Order of Importance, Reasons Why
- Most to Least; top 10 list, ie. David Letterman 10, 9, 8, etc.)
- Dewey Decimal System (100, 200, 300, etc.)
- Chronology

Analyze Strategies

- What is it? (structure) How is it used? (function)
- Strength, Weakness
- Compare, Contrast, or Similarities, Differences
- Good News, Bad News,
- Yes, No
- Backward, Forward
- Pros, Cons
- Problem, Action, Result (PAR)
- Strengths, Weaknesses, Opportunities, Threats
- Profit, Sales, Market Share, Growth
- Situation, Task, Action, Result (STAR)
- Well, Maybe, But...
- Formal/Informal

PERSUASIVE

Order Strategies

- Order of Importance, Reasons Why
- Most to Least; top 10 list, ie. David Letterman 10, 9, 8, etc.)

Analyze Strategies

- Problem, Solution
- Features, Benefits
- Possibilities, Consequences
- Do's, Don'ts
- Before, After
- Pros, Cons
- Causes, Effects
- Reasons, Alternatives
- Works, Doesn't Work
- Good News, Bad News,
- Yes, No
- Good, Bad, Ugly
- Good, Better, Best, Yes, No, Maybe; Problem, Action, Result (PAR)
- Monroe's Motivated Sequence
  - Attention
  - Need
  - Satisfaction
  - Visualization
  - Action
- What it is (structure)?
- Why is it important (functionality)?
- Well, Maybe, But...
- Formal/Informal

Library Scavenger Hunt

Complete this fun activity to locate credible sources for your speech. When you complete the process outlined in the Library Scavenger Hunt you will have the resources you need to write your speech. Be sure that you complete your reference list as you accumulate the sources.

1. Review the libary resources for your topic and be sure to play with various "research" words that will help your search.

2. Cite your source on your reference page (begin your reference page now or insert into your speech at www. speechformula.com).

3. Locate your sources.
    a. Define your topic using an encyclopedia if not available. use a dictionary. (Try to avoid a .com).
    b. Search the circulation desk to see if any actual books are in the library which you can use. (Check e-books too.)
    c. Search the databases available through the library to see what is available on your topic.
    d. Are there any interesting quotes regarding your topic? Search quote books or quote websites.

4. Speak with a librarian to see if they can provide additional insight in your search. Briefly explain their comments.

5. Do you need further research to complete this speech?

6. Print out your references as needed for your Informative Speech..

7.6 Your Source Credibility

How can you identify if information is credible or not on the internet? Conduct an internet search on this question and see what criteria you can identify. Establish a plan to ensure that you will check your information to determine if it is credible. Change as needed for your speech.

Plan   Step 1:

Step 2:

Step 3:

Use our web application: www.credibilitychecker.com

Who is the **author**?

☐ Widely-cited Author(s)

☐ Credentialed Author(s)

☐ Famous Author(s)

☐ Author(s) not known

☐ Does the author have a slant or known bias?

When was it published?

☐ Within 5 years

☐ Over 5 years but seminal work

☐ Over 5 years but historical use

☐ Date unknown

What type of **citations** are featured?

☐ Reference page or Footnotes

☐ Statistics, reference, raw data source

☐ None

How **credible** is the information?

☐ Primary

☐ Secondary
  · Study of studies
  · Paraphrased

Who **published** the source?

☐ **3rd Party**
Peer Reviewed
Academic Books
Mainstream Media
  · Respected Publisher
  · Major Newspaper
  · Popular Magazine
  · Local Newspaper
Government Publication
Professional (Industry) Publication

☐ **Self Published** Book
Company Publication or Website
Printed Pamphlet
Edited Community Website
Wiki Page
Individual Blog

☐ Does the publisher have a slant or known bias?

7.7 4 Ps for a Perfect Speech (Connect)

Suppose you had to give a speech on the topic of "travel." Provide a creative, engaging example of how you would incorporate each of the four Ps for a perfect speech.

Sample 4 Ps Applied to Speech Topic

CONNECTION	HOW WILL YOU?
Probing Question	
Prop	
Physical Activity	
Personal Story	

4 Ps

For each type of connection listed below, explain how you will engage your audience by creating the specific type of connection. Be creative, do your best, your audience will be sure to appreciate your effort.

Personal Story: Personal stories should be specific and relevant to the topic and point you are trying to make. They should strengthen your speech. Be sure to include names, dates, and places. Careful that the story itself does not overpower your speech to replace your purpose, it is easy to do. At the end of the speech the stories should make your purpose make sense not distract from it. One good way to test is to practice the speech — ask the practice what are the points of the speech? If they refer to the story, it overpowered your points — be sure to use your story to make your points not distract. Each speech of any substance should contain a meaningful personal story as a way to reveal who you are to the audience and create a personal connection.

Probing Questions: Ask very clear, specific questions that guide the audience to consider the point you are trying to make. Sometimes you can ask questions that lead the audience to an experience they have in their mind which they can then connect to the content. For example: Who is the happiest person you know? Who is the most miserable? How happy are you? For a speech on happiness, this guides the audience to consider their need to be happier. Other times you can ask probing questions to get the audience to internalize the content you are sharing. If you show a list of ten items you can ask the audience to identify the item that they identify with in some way.

Prop: Use props to make the insert the ideas and content into the audience. Some topics allow for a literal display to represent the ideas, sometimes we need to get creative on how to create these and ignite our audience with the content. For example: Hold up a book you reference, create cards with key words that you infuse into the audience or into an interaction or activity, you can also share charts or pictures. I encourage speakers to use infuse two dimensional objects rather than only relying upon a video or image on the screen — variety grasps attention.

Physical Activity: Interaction allows the audience to have an experience rather than a lecture. Every speech should require at least two butts out of seats. Simply asking yes or no question by asking them to stand for the answer. There are so many creative ways that you can get the audience to move, most of the time this movement is a wonderful way to engage and create powerful connections.

CONNECTION	ADVICE
Personal Story	Personal stories should be specific, relevant to the topic, and strengthen your speech in some way. They should include names, dates, and places. Be sure they do not overpower your speech to become the focus. Remember it is not about you, but about breaking the information down so the research makes sense to the audience and the story creates a personal connection. **Be careful to keep the story brief for a short speech.**
Probing Questions	Get the audience to think about your topic in a way that's relevant to them. Consider all topic perspectives.
Prop	Make sure the prop is relevant to the topic and will help your speech. Ex: books, videos, pictures, charts.
Physical Activity	Get the audience to interact with your speech. Get them moving and active. Ask them to answer questions, write things down, move to a place in the classroom.

Sample 4 Ps Applied to Speech Topic

CONNECTION	HOW WILL YOU?
Probe	
Prop	
Physical	
Personal Story	

7.8 Conclusion

Write the conclusion for your speech topic.*

Review the Main Points:

Restate Thesis:

Support:

State:

Relate:

Return to Attention Introduction:

Refer to the sample speech throughout the chapter if you have any questions filling out the Formula. To simplify the process use the the application at www.speechplan.com.

Category	Definition	Strategy for Main Points
NAME Topical Label Classification	Term for identification. Names can identify a class or category of things or a single thing either uniquely or with a given context.	When we begin the organization process, identification begins by naming. Once named, one can then decide if a system of organization will help to create clearer meaning to our audience. Objects or ideas can be organized by placing in a particular order or by analyzing features of the object or idea. We have the freedom to organize our ideas in an infinite number of ways. It is important for the designer of the message to consider the available options and choose the one the works best for what it is you are trying to do.
ORDER Numerical Alphabetical Chronological Rank Spatial Logical	Arranging ideas, objects or people in relation to each other according to a particular sequence, pattern or method.	Typically, speeches that strive for a lower persuasive appeal and less emotion lend themselves to using an order strategy to organize the content. NOTE: Exceptions exist, for instance an announcement (informative) typically uses Analysis of 5 criteria, Who, What, Where, When and Why. Both informative and persuasive speeches can use a sequential numerical strategy. The 3 Basic Principles About Exercise (Informative). The 3 Reasons Why You Should Begin An Exercise Routine Today (Persuasive).
Numerical	Expressed as a number or numbers. Often ideas are driven by steps or need, therefore we represent the ideas with a number to assign meaning to the logical placement. Using numbers can help.	• Sequential (1,2,3), • Motivated Sequence (Step 1, Step 2, Step 3) • Order of Importance (Most or Least) (Top 10 List - • David Letterman 10, 9, 8 etc.) • Dewey Decimal System (100 , 200, 300, etc)

Alphabetical	A system whereby strings of characters are placed in order based on the position of the characters in the conventional ordering of an alphabet.	Letter (A, B, C)
Chronology	The arrangement of events or dates in the order of their occurrence.	• Timeline (1800, 1900, 2000) • Era, (Big Band, Rock, Hip Hop) • Schedule (Morning, Afternoon, Evening)
Rank	Relative position, value, worth complexity, power, importance, authority or level in the hierarchy of a given system.	• Military (General, Captain, Lieutenant) • Corporate (President, Vice President, Manager) • Government (President, Vice President, Secretary)
Spatial	Of or relating to space.	• Direction (I. North, II. South, III. East, IV. West) • Orientation (I. Top II. Middle III. Bottom) (Head/Shoulders Knees, Toes) • I. Internal II. External (Inside/Outside) • I. Vertical (Y) II. Horizontal (X) • I. Backward II. Forward
Logical	A reasonable or sensible way that something happens or would happen.	• I. Ingredients, II. Utensils, III. Directions; • Color: I. Blue II. Red • Size: I. Small II. Medium III.Large • I. General II. Specific
ANALYZE 2 Criteria 3 Criteria 4 Criteria 5 Criteria	Discover or reveal through detailed explanation. Examine methodically the constitution or structure of something.	Typically, speeches that strive for a higher persuasive appeal and greater emotion achieve that by identifying an organizational strategy that analyzes the content. Analysis allows our message to reveal relationships or lack of coherence with the given topic. Using these strategies effectively can serve to empower your message significantly. NOTE: Exceptions exist, for instance an announcement (informative) typically uses Analysis of 5 criteria, Who, What, Where, When and Why. Both informative and persuasive speeches can use a sequential numerical strategy. The 3 Basic Principles About Exercise (Informative). The 3 Reasons Why You Should Begin An Exercise Routine Today (Persuasive).

2 Criteria	Analyzing content by examining two different criteria in order to reveal specific features of the object or idea.	I. Problem II. Solution I. Features II. Benefits I. What it is (Structure) ? II. How it is used (Function)? I. Possibilities II. Consequences I. Do's II. Don'ts I. Before II. After I. Pros II. Cons I. Strengths II. Weakness I. Causes II. Effects I. Reasons II. Alternatives, I. Compare II. Contrast or I. Similarities II.Differences I. Works II. Doesn't Work I. Good News II. Bad NewsI. Yes II. No I. Backwards II. Forward I. Macro (Big Picture) II. Micro (Small Picture)
3 Criteria	Analyzing content by examining three different criteria in order to reveal specific features of the object or idea.	I. Good II. Bad,III. Ugly; I. Good II.Better III. Best I. Yes II. No III. Maybe; I. Problem II. Action III. Result (PAR)
4 Criteria	Analyzing content by examining four different criteria in order to reveal specific features of the object or idea.	I. Strengths, II. Weaknesses, III. Opportunities, IV. Threats I. Profit II. Sales III. Market Share IV. Growth I. Situation II. Task III. Action IV Result (STAR)

5 Criteria	Analyzing content by examining five different criteria in order to reveal specific features of the object or idea.	I. Who II. What III. Where, IV. Why IV. When
		
		Monroe's Motivated Sequence
		
		    1. Attention
		    2. Need
		    3. Satisfaction
		    4. Visualization
		    5. Action

7.9 Introduction

Write the introduction for your speech topic.*

Thesis

Relate:

State:

Support:

Preview the Main Points:

7.10 Conclusion

Write the conclusion for your speech topic.*

Review the Main Points:

Restate Thesis:

Support:

State:

Relate:

Return to Attention Grabber:

Chapter 7 Review Questions

1. What are the five parts to a dynamic speech?

2. Describe the three different types of audience anayalysis.

3. What are the five rules for writing a quality purpose statement?

4. Which part of the speech is most important to you, the audience?

5. Which part of the speech is most imporant to you, the author? Why?

6. Who writes the speech?

7. What order do you use to deliver the speech?

8. In what order do you construct the speech?

9. Suppose you were delivering a speech with this purpose statement: By the end of my speech my audience create a great personal brand. Identify three organizational strategies you could use. Which would work best?

10. How are the introduction and conclusion different?

11. How many times should you tell your audience your main points during the course of the speech?

12. Which quote from this chapter resonates with you the most?

Sample Speech: Randy Pausch, Really Achieving Your Childhood Dreams

1. Watch Randy Pausch's speech, *Really Achieving Your Childhood Dreams*: http://www.cmu.edu/randyslecture/

2. Analyze his speech:

   a. Outline his speech (use an outline not an essay).

   b. Compare/contrast the outline of Professor Pausch's speech to the Speech Formula you used to write the speech in this chapter. Did Dr. Pausch follow the Speech Formula? What was the same? What was different?

   c. In your opinion what were the best moments of his speech? What were the weakest moments? Why?

   d. Consultation: Suppose you had the opportunity to consult with him prior to delivering his speech again to an even larger crowd, what advice would you offer him? What should he do the same? What should he do differently?

> Organizing is what you do before you do something, so that when you do it, it is not all mixed up.
>
> – A.A. Milne

Chapter 8:
Putting It All Together

Objectives

By the end of this chapter you should be able to:

1. Compare and contrast the two components of a great speech.

2. Explain the significance of the design of the message.

3. Identify the three stages involved in the design of the speech according to the Construction Checklist?

4. State the components of the delivery strategy?

5. Create an effective personal plan of action.

Formula Test

How well do you know the formula?

1. The questions on your Primary Audience analysis come from …?
2. Do you formally ask your audience the Primary Audience Analysis questions?
3. Should the questions you construct refer to your topic? Why or Why not?
4. What is a question that you should ask when conducting your secondary formal audience analysis?
5. What part of the speech is **most** important to **you** the **author**? Why?
6. What part of the speech is **most** important to the **audience**? Why?
7. Who writes the speech?
8. What determines the success of your speech (3 things)?
9. In what order should you write/construct your speech?
10. In what order should you deliver your speech?
11. Where should you begin using the outline format?
12. Which part of the body drives the speech?
13. What crucial step must you do with your research prior to constructing your body?
14. Identify 3 methods to organize and 2 corresponding organizational strategies (where applicable) you might use when constructing a speech.
15. Using vacation as your topic, provide an example of what might be a main point and a sub point. Determine your methodology and desired organizational strategy.
16. Describe at least 3 functions of the main points.
17. Describe at least 3 functions of a sub point.
18. Identify where and how 3 persuasive appeals should be used in your introduction during your thesis.
19. What should a good example contain? Provide a good example of a good example!
20. Identify 5 rules for using power points in your presentation.
21. Describe what your cards should contain.
22. Which part of the formula do you least understand?
23. How many times should you read your speech out loud before you move to cards?
24. What is the biggest mistake people make with cards?

Write the **Formula** for Delivering a Dynamic Speech as outlined on the first page of your Speech Evaluation Form. Be sure to use the outline format where appropriate.

APPENDIXES

Construction Checklist   Fill this out as you proceed through each step

Check	Stage One & Two: Planning & Preparation	Process

	Topic
	Remember: the audience writes the speech!
	Audience Analysis: Who is my audience? How do they think? Why?
	Secondary: 1. Why is this topic important to them?
	                    2. How will my audience benefit from my words?
	                    3. Will they learn something new?
		Ask questions re:
		demographics, psychographics or behavioral.

	Research Quality research adds credibility. Primary not secondary (hearsay). Who created content? Who paid for it, why? Need *author and date*. Create reference page first; share sources *verbally and visually*	**Plagiarism = crime** No Wikipedia Journals are great Peer reviewed is great
	Establish a Purpose Statement Consider: audience analysis/research/your goal—be crystal clear!	**Wash cycle** (work out the dirt, have clean, clear thoughts)
	Construct a Skeleton Outline Determine organizational strategy. Write *only* main points and sub points.	**Consider the logic!** Refer to organizational matrix
	Stage Three: Construction	
	Outline *Audience Analysis, Purpose Statement, Body, Intro, Conclusion* Fill in the Formula. Begin with body, take skeleton outline and fill in with full sentences including your research and examples. Speech writes itself!	**Do *not* use essay format.**
	Quotes/Questions/Transitions Include: quote to illustrate a point, questions posed to audience, clear guidance from point to point. Act like a tour guide guiding audience from point to point.	Search for famous quotes on your topic, stretches speech!
	Check for Mistakes, Did you... Stretch, knockout, preview, fallacy, examples, conclude	Make it right, don't leave it wrong!
	Peer Review Have buddy read and provide meaningful feedback.	Sign off:
	Stage Four: Delivery	
	1. Read Read your speech out loud 5-10 times.	Benefit: you won't have to memorize.
	2. Create Your Cards & Visuals Cards = **Formula** + Key Words *only*	Too many words = reading too much = no connection.
	Visuals: Presentation Aids (Powerpoint) • Use key words... no full sentences. Everything supports purpose • No FUNK (fonts, colors, sounds, timing, movement, distracting images) • 1st slide preview main points; no intro slide. Back up (jpg & 200) • Practice/coordinate with buddy. Do not read slides interact, engage. • Bring handouts for audience. Include references. Print hard copy.	**C.R.A.P. Concept:** Consistency, Repetition Alignment, Proximity See: The Non-Designer's Design Book by Robin Williams
	3. Practice, Practice, Practice Principles: __Set the Stage, __Speak Up, __Stretch, __Energy, __Audience Connection, __Pauses, __Time, __Space Verbal: __Projection, __Speed, __Pronunciation, __Enunciation, __Emphasis Nonverbal: __Professional dress, __Eye contact, __Hand gestures, __Posture, __Smile	What are your strengths and weaknesses? Develop an **Action Plan.**

	Action Plan: My personal delivery goals are:
	    1.
	    2.
	    3.
		Always ask:
		Did I incorporate the delivery principles?

	4. Audio/Video Analysis: (Record yourself w/cell phone and critique). You are your best critic. Assess your Strengths/Weaknesses/Opportunities/Threats	If you don't, it's like going on a date without looking in the mirror.
	Time: *Do* Eliminate Words; *Don't* Speak Faster Never rush your delivery; everything takes longer live.	Practice Time:

Speech Formula Checklist Provides a Systematic Method to Develop a Dynamic Speech

Formula	Score	Comments - Any Mistakes?
Audience Analysis		
Primary: Ask 5 specific questions regarding the audience demographics, psychographics or behaviors.		
Secondary: Connect speaker, message and audience. 1. Why is this topic important to **them**? 2. How will my audience **benefit** from my words? 3. Will they learn something **new**?		Get in the heart and mind of your audience. Speak from an audience-centered perspective.
Formal: Explore what your audience thinks and feels about your topic. Include the data in your presentation as an effective strategy to connect the content to their specific needs. Construct 5–10 questions you can ask the audience regarding your topic.		
Purpose Statement: Establishes a clear goal!		
Follow these 5 rules to develop your Purpose Statement: 1. Use words, "By the end of my speech my audience will…" 2. Dream! **Go Big!** What would you like to occur? 3. Keep it simple: 1 idea, no ands or conjunctions 4. Use active verbs—something you can physically do 5. Do not share with audience. This is only for you.		
Introduction: Convinces the audience to listen.		TOPIC LEVEL ONLY
Attention Grabber Interesting and provocative. Have them at "Hello!" Stretch.		Activity, movie clip Stands out, different from the rest.
Thesis 1. Relate (pathos): Appeal to audience, ask questions. 2. State (logos): - Propose (the logical argument or thesis statement) 3. Support (ethos): Speaker credentials, authoritative quotations, statistics		Don't go into information from points or research of your speech—only introduce the idea with statements supporting the topic.
Preview Main Points One sentence; literally copy/past your main points.		**Repetition is good.** Audience should remember.
Body: Reveals valuable information about the topic.		USE ROMAN NUMERALS HERE
Which organizational strategy works best to support the purpose? Main points: _____ Sub points: _____		
I./II. Main Point (must have 2 main points) Breaks down topic; category title for sub points. Should be easy to remember, organized		Too many words = reading too much = no connection.
A./B. Sub Point (must have 2 sub points) Provides name (description) for your research like "Definition" or "Types". Breaks down main point.		
1. **Source:** Drives the speech; reveal "jewels" of information you have discovered. Share/cite source (display on PP cite orally/paper/PP).		
2. **Connection:** 4Ps = Super Speech (Personal Story, Probing Questions, Physical Activity, Prop) What type of connection will you select to connect with your audience? The 4 Ps are crucial to help your audience make sense of the information.		What type of connection are you using? Engage audience, make it make sense!
Transitions/Connectors/Sign Posts Act as a tour guide, explaining where you are and where you are going.		Don't be afraid to share your organization.
Conclusion: Remind them why they listened.		Introduction backwards
Review main points *"Today we discussed…"* Review thesis. Include: Relate, State, Support Return to Attention Grabber.		Share main points not sub points. Return to each part. Bring them full circle.
Call to Action: Include a persuasive appeal that is timely and specific.		**Only Persuasive Speech.**

Practice. Deliver. Reflect.

This section is devoted to providing you the tools to advance your delivery. Rarely will anyone judge you as harshly as you judge yourself. A good delivery takes time, allow ample time to represent yourself well.

Practice

1. Read your speech out loud 5-10 times until the words fall off your tongue.
2. Think carefully about the response you want from your audience, what do you need to do to get it?
3. Consider each delivery principle, carefully plan where and how you will incorporate the principle you wish to implement.
4. Use notecards.
5. Use a mirror until you become comfortable and feel ready to deliver. Listen to your voice using a recorder.
6. Video yourself in front of people (cell phones work great). Critique the video, identifying strengths, weaknesses, opportunities and threats.
7. Check out the room you will deliver. PRACTICE—electronic equipment.

Deliver

1. Have the entire presentation ready the night before the delivery. Everything printed, handouts, files, any Plan "B" —so you don't add stress to an already stressful situation.
2. DRESS. Your confidence will soar if you look the part. Dressing is a sign of respect for your audience.
3. Remember to "Set the Stage" from the time you enter the premises until you leave. Be prepared, composed. If you have a "buddy" don't talk to them focus on audience. Grab each audience member's attention before you begin.
4. Visualize how the words might impact the audience, be confident in yourself but focus on the audience rather than your own nerves.
5. Be sure to breath, relax, have fun!
6. Make first words meaningful, don't use filler words!
7. Video the presentation (cell phone).

Reflect

1. Review audience feedback.
2. Review your own impressions of the presentation.
3. Review the video.
4. Record your strengths, weaknesses, opportunities and threats that you and your audience observed.
5. Create a Plan of Action you will integrate into your next speech to develop your communication skills.

Reflection Process

Evaluating a Speech

The evaluation process is crucial to your development as a speaker.

1. **Hand out feedback sheets:** Before you deliver a speech pass around the Speech Feedback sheets to at least 3 audience members. These individuals should critique your delivery independent of the class feedback.
2. **Record you speech.** Be sure to give your cell phone to a buddy to record your delivery. One of the most beneficial ways to improve as a speaker is to be willing to literally look at yourself delivering.
3. **Analyze data:** Review your video, review the feedback provided by your audience. Carefully consider all of it.
4. **Complete the Speech Reflection Journal on the next page.** Below is a sample Plan of Action you will use to develop your public speaking skills.

Final Question (This question will appear on your final): As you progress through this book you have maintained a journal of your development as a speaker both in your speech reflection journals and on the diary of the video recordings of your speeches. Review both archives. Describe key points along your journey. Explain how this awareness helped you improve. Explore what you saw in the videos: was the feedback the same as your perception of your performance? Who evaluated whom more harshly? What do you now know about yourself as a speaker?

Improvement Plan

#	Performance Goal	Detailed Plan
Goal #1	Set the Stage	1. Prepare well, know my first lines, and visualize success. 2. Breathe, stand straight, demonstrating with my body language the confidence from my preparation. Look at the audience, listen to their non-verbal communication, wait for them settle and lean forward to listen. 3. Deliver the first line without looking down—establish eye contact
Goal #2	Increase audience connection	1. 2. 3.
Goal #3	Stretch the bandwidth of my speech	1. 2. 3.

Note: Once you have outlined your goals and how you plan to achieve them, be sure to integrate your plan into your next speech. Write each goal where it will happen in the speech. For instance 1.1, 1.2, 1.3 goes before the first words of the speech.

Self Reflection Journal Speech for: _____

Assess your performance on the speech you delivered by answering these questions.

1. How well prepared were you to deliver your speech?
    - ☐ I read it out loud 10 times, practiced in front of a mirror, used my cell phone to see my delivery and made the appropriate adjustments to improve.
    - ☐ I read my cards and practiced in the mirror, but wish I had worked a bit more.
    - ☐ I read my cards but could have worked to make conscious adjustments before I got in front of my audience.
    - ☐ I read the speech once or twice.
    - ☐ I am writing my cards out in class.

2. How well did you feel that you did delivering your speech?
    - ☐ Nailed it! I seriously ROCK!
    - ☐ I did good, there were a few things I wish had happened more like how I practiced them.
    - ☐ Wow… there are so many things I wanted to do that didn't go how I planned.
    - ☐ I could have done better, I'm so pissed!
    - ☐ Why did I even bother to get out of bed… HELP!

3. What feedback did you receive from your audience? (Give a number to each.)

    ___ Set the Stage   ___ Sweeten It!   ___ Speak Up   ___ Time   ___ Energy

    ___ Space   ___ Pause   ___ Dance   ___ Engage   ___ Have Fun

4. How similar or different was your audience feedback from your own opinion? How distorted were the two versions?

5. Create a delivery plan of action. Watch the video of your delivery and consider all the feedback and what you have learned about the delivery goals. Select 3 delivery goals you intend to focus on for your next speech. Be sure to select these from your list of Delivery Principles for your next speech and explain with at least 3 specific steps for each delivery principle goal.

#	Goal	Steps	Evaluator #1-10
1		1. 2. 3.	
2		1. 2. 3.	
3		1. 2. 3.	

Self Reflection Journal Speech

Assess your performance on the speech you delivered by answering these questions.

1. How well prepared were you to deliver your speech?
   - ☐ I read it out loud 10 times, practiced in front of a mirror, used my cell phone to see my delivery and made the appropriate adjustments to improve.
   - ☐ I read my cards and practiced in the mirror, but wish I had worked a bit more.
   - ☐ I read my cards but could have worked to make conscious adjustments before I got in front of my audience.
   - ☐ I read the speech once or twice.
   - ☐ I am writing my cards out in class.

2. How well did you feel that you did delivering your speech?
   - ☐ Nailed it! I seriously ROCK!
   - ☐ I did good, there were a few things I wish had happened more like how I practiced them.
   - ☐ Wow... there are so many things I wanted to do that didn't go how I planned.
   - ☐ I could have done better, I'm so pissed!
   - ☐ Why did I even bother to get out of bed... HELP!

3. What feedback did you receive from your audience? (Give a number to each.)

   ___ Set the Stage   ___ Sweeten It!   ___ Speak Up   ___ Time   ___ Energy

   ___ Space   ___ Pause   ___ Dance   ___ Engage   ___ Have Fun

4. How similar or different was your audience feedback from your own opinion? How distorted were the two versions?

5. Create a delivery plan of action. Watch the video of your delivery and consider all the feedback and what you have learned about the delivery goals. Select 3 delivery goals you intend to focus on for your next speech. Be sure to select these from your list of Delivery Principles for your next speech and explain with at least 3 specific steps for each delivery principle goal.

#	Goal	Steps	Evaluator #1-10
1		1. 2. 3.	
2		1. 2. 3.	
3		1. 2. 3.	

Self Reflection Journal Speech

Assess your performance on the speech you delivered by answering these questions.

1. How well prepared were you to deliver your speech?
   - ☐ I read it out loud 10 times, practiced in front of a mirror, used my cell phone to see my delivery and made the appropriate adjustments to improve.
   - ☐ I read my cards and practiced in the mirror, but wish I had worked a bit more.
   - ☐ I read my cards but could have worked to make conscious adjustments before I got in front of my audience.
   - ☐ I read the speech once or twice.
   - ☐ I am writing my cards out in class.

2. How well did you feel that you did delivering your speech?
   - ☐ Nailed it! I seriously ROCK!
   - ☐ I did good, there were a few things I wish had happened more like how I practiced them.
   - ☐ Wow... there are so many things I wanted to do that didn't go how I planned.
   - ☐ I could have done better, I'm so pissed!
   - ☐ Why did I even bother to get out of bed... HELP!

3. What feedback did you receive from your audience? (Give a number to each.)

   ___ Set the Stage   ___ Sweeten It!   ___ Speak Up   ___ Time   ___ Energy

   ___ Space   ___ Pause   ___ Dance   ___ Engage   ___ Have Fun

4. How similar or different was your audience feedback from your own opinion? How distorted were the two versions?

5. Create a delivery plan of action. Watch the video of your delivery and consider all the feedback and what you have learned about the delivery goals. Select 3 delivery goals you intend to focus on for your next speech. Be sure to select these from your list of Delivery Principles for your next speech and explain with at least 3 specific steps for each delivery principle goal.

#	Goal	Steps	Evaluator #1-10
1		1. 2. 3.	
2		1. 2. 3.	
3		1. 2. 3.	

Speech Feedback Form

Beginning Speech: _____

Strengths

1.

2.

3.

Weaknesses

1.

2.

Comments:

Grade: **A B C D F**   Instructions: Yes / No

Citation: Yes / No

Delivery Principles 1-10:

___ Set the Stage   ___ Sweeten It!   ___ Speak Up

___ Time   ___ Energy   ___ Space

___ Pause   ___ Dance   ___ Engage

___ Have Fun

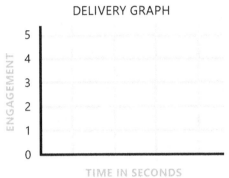

Speech Feedback Form

Beginning Speech: _____

Strengths

1.

2.

3.

Weaknesses

1.

2.

Comments:

Grade: **A B C D F**   Instructions: Yes / No

Citation: Yes / No

Delivery Principles 1-10:

___ Set the Stage   ___ Sweeten It!   ___ Speak Up

___ Time   ___ Energy   ___ Space

___ Pause   ___ Dance   ___ Engage

___ Have Fun

DELIVERY GRAPH

Speech Feedback Form

Advanced Speech: _____

Strengths

1.

2.

3.

Weaknesses

1.

2.

Comments:

Grade: **A B C D F**   Instructions: Yes / No

Citation: Yes / No

Delivery Principles 1-10:

__ Set the Stage	__ Sweeten It!	__ Speak Up
__ Time	__ Energy	__ Space
__ Pause	__ Dance	__ Engage
__ Have Fun		

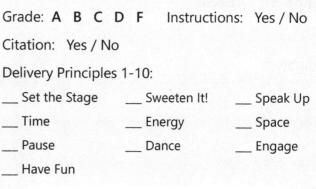

DELIVERY GRAPH

Speech Feedback Form

Advanced Speech: _____

Strengths

1.

2.

3.

Weaknesses

1.

2.

Comments:

Grade: **A B C D F**   Instructions: Yes / No

Citation: Yes / No

Delivery Principles 1-10:

__ Set the Stage	__ Sweeten It!	__ Speak Up
__ Time	__ Energy	__ Space
__ Pause	__ Dance	__ Engage
__ Have Fun		

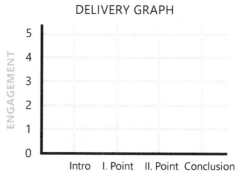

DELIVERY GRAPH

Persuasive/Informative Performance

Indicate how you have implemented course content in your delivery of these speeches.

#	Question	Informative	Persuasive
1	**Sources:** How many sources did you cite?	Oral _____ In text _____ Visual _____ Reference_____ (Indicate rating 1-5 for each source.)	Oral _____ In text _____ Visual _____ Reference_____ (Indicate rating 1-5 for each source.)
	How credible were your sources? (#Stars*)	#1___ 2___ 3___ 4___ 5___ (Indicate rating Y/N for each of 5 sources.)	#1___ 2___ 3___ 4___ 5___ (Indicate rating Y/N for each of 5 sources.)
	Did you share why your sources are credible to your audience?	#1___ 2___ 3___ 4___ 5___	#1___ 2___ 3___ 4___ 5___
2	**Purpose:** How many of the 5 rules did you follow?	1 2 3 4 5 (circle)	1 2 3 4 5 (circle)
3	**Organization:** Which organizational strategy did you select to best meet your purpose?	_____ _____	_____ _____
	Was strategy make purpose happen?	Yes No	Yes No
4	**Connection:** Degree of Creativity (1-10)	_____	_____
	Physical (physically engage audience)	Awesome OK Weak NA	Awesome OK Weak NA
	Props (Object engage audience)	Awesome OK Weak NA	Awesome OK Weak NA
	Probe (questions conjure their story)	Awesome OK Weak NA	Awesome OK Weak NA
5	**Visuals:** Did you follow the rules for using visuals? (1 lowest - 5 highest)	1 2 3 4 5 (circle)	1 2 3 4 5 (circle)
	Creation		
	Key words only	Yes No	Yes No
	Words/colors legible/support purpose	1 2 3 4 5 (circle)	1 2 3 4 5 (circle)
	Information cited (APA)	1 2 3 4 5 (circle)	1 2 3 4 5 (circle)
	Main points: preview/body/review	preview___ body___ review___	preview___ body___ review___
	Explain any images/consistent	Yes No	Yes No
	Have back up (email & thumb drive)	email___ thumb___ prints___	email___ thumb___ prints___
	Delivery		
	Don't read word for word	1___ 2___ 3___ 4___ 5___	1___ 2___ 3___ 4___ 5___
	Interact each slide call audience member (fewer than 1/3 slide)	1___ 2___ 3___ 4___ 5___	1___ 2___ 3___ 4___ 5___
	Have printout of slides for audience	Yes No	Yes No

6	**Notecards:** To what extent did you follow the rules for note cards? Formula Only key words Research not on cards only visual	1 2 3 4 5 (circle) Yes No Yes No Yes No	

7	**Introduction:**
	To what extent did you employ the elements of the Introduction?
	Attention Grabber
	Thesis: Relate (questions/probe)
	      State (purpose statement)
	      Support
	Preview main points
		1 2 3 4 5 (circle)
		
		Awesome OK Weak
		Yes No
		(direct) Yes No
		(quote) Yes No
		Yes No
			1 2 3 4 5 (circle)
			
			Awesome OK Weak
			Yes No
			(gentle) Yes No
			(law) Yes No
			Yes No

8	**Conclusion:** Did you return briefly to each point of your introduction? How cool was your call to action? (Persuasive)	Yes No	Yes No Awesome OK Weak
9	**Evaluation:** The *best* part of my speech was... The *weakest* part of my speech was... What would you do differently?	_____ _____ _____	_____ _____ _____

Made in the USA
Columbia, SC
14 January 2020